C000001495

Published by GorillaPhysics in the UK

ISBN-13: 9798611258545

2020

© Kit Betts-Masters

Contents

| | i. | This Book | 6 |
| | ii. | More about the Challenge of A Level Physics | 9 |

1.	Introduction to A Level Topics	10
	i.	Mechanics	11
	ii.	DC Electricity	16
	iii.	Materials	19
	iv.	Waves	20
	v.	Quantum	22
	vi.	Further Mechanics	25
	vii.	Simple Harmonic Motion	28
	viii.	Particle Physics	29
	ix.	Electromagnetism	31
	x.	Nuclear Physics	32
	xi.	Gravitational Fields	34
	xii.	Thermal Physics	35
	xiii.	Astrophysics	37
	xiv.	Practical Physics	41

2.	Three "Try This at Home" Experiments	43
	i.	Video Analysis	44
	ii.	Time Period of a Pendulum	52
	iii.	Half Life of a Two Litre Bottle of Water	60

3.		Independent Study Tasks	67
	i.	Projectile Simulations	68
	ii.	Feynman on Energy	70
	iii.	Measure Viscosity	71
	iv.	Reading Lists	78
	v.	Explainer Video of an Experiment	80
	vi.	Timeline of the Theory of Light	86
	vii.	Review Exam Papers with Examiners Reports	90
	viii.	Measure Specific Heat Capacity of Water	91
	ix.	Measure the Diameter of the Sun and the Moon	93
	x.	Make a Flowchart of the History of Astrophysics	96
	xi.	Coulomb's Law Practical	98
	xii.	Make an Academic Poster	101
	xiii.	Write Your Own Difficult Context Based Questions	103
	xiv.	Make a Timeline of Particle Physics	106
	xv.	Compare the Impact of Newton and Einstein	107
	xvi.	Annotate Your Equation Sheet	109
	xvii.	Review Last Year's Examiners Reports	112
	xviii.	Make Revision Cards for Exam Questions on Experiments	114
	xix.	Extra Independent Tasks	116
4.		Most Importantly….	122
	i.	Feedback is Always Welcome and Always Useful	123
	ii.	Thanks and Acknowledgements	124

This Book

This book is about getting excited! Physics is the most challenging A Level, but it's the most interesting one as well. The fact that you've chosen A Level Physics is a good sign, you've shown an interest in how the Universe works and you aren't afraid of a little bit of intense study to get that understanding. If you only get one thing from this book, I hope it's an enthusiasm and an excitement for what you are about to find out.

There's no pressure with this book, it's not directly linked to any syllabus and there's no test at the end. I've written you some really challenging tasks, and some really accessible ones as well, and any time I've written you a question, I've provided a step by step answer!

There are three main sections; introductions to each topic in the A Level, three in depth experiments for you to conduct and analyse at home, and a set of tasks that should give you things to do to keep you motivated and challenge you to work at the highest level throughout the two years of A Level.

In the topic introductions I've tried to give you a heads up as to what's hard about each one, but also an insight into what's fascinating about the topic. There are no boring topics in A Level Physics, ignore anyone who tells you "this is just a boring bit that you have to learn a lot of details." Look past that, everything we've included in GCSE or A Level we've put there because it's fascinating and important.

Whenever you start to ask yourself *can I be bothered to study this?* Stop. Put down your text book, come back to one of the tasks in this book. A little reading, watching a few videos on the cutting-edge research in that area of physics, will bring you back to enjoying your study.

Enjoying your study is the ~~best~~ only way to make it effective!

The three in depth experiments should be easy enough to conduct at home and still get valid results! You should be able to find everything you need in the home or otherwise at very low cost at the supermarket.

You will meet your own challenges in conducting these experiments! The problems you must solve will be specific to you, your apparatus, and your context. Handling data, coming up with practical solutions, improving experimental techniques and coming up with new and interesting ways to investigate theory, are the best bits of learning physics at A level! Engaging with this type of higher-level thinking is the most effective way to prepare to handle the challenges in Physics exams.

I've given you an approximate method for each practical and some ideas to get you thinking about some of the problems the experiments will introduce. Importantly these activities will give you a taste of some of the analytical techniques that you will need to use every day in your Physics lessons.

I then ask some questions to help you think around the theories that the experiments develop. Some of the questions are related to your experiment directly whilst some are related to similar experiments or related theories. Some are calculations for which you need to research the equations if you don't already know them, and some will need quite extensive research for you to answer them and they could become more extended writing tasks.

I have given answers to these questions but trust yourself to answer these questions completely before you look at the answers. I always think that textbooks should have answers to the questions, but it is a waste of your time to look at answers without thinking through the problems. Make sure you have a good go yourself before checking and improving your response with the answers! Don't worry even if your answer is way off mine, thinking and effort is never wasted. The answers are just there so that you aren't left wondering afterwards, and that when you have struggled, and still can't figure it out, you get a complete learning experience by being shown the answer.

Lastly for the experiments, a note about safety. These experiments contain few hazards and very low risk, but you should get into the habit of assessing the risk yourself before conducting any practical activities. If you are planning something beyond the experiments as set out here, just have a quick conversation about keeping safe with a responsible person, as they may consider things that you have not thought about.

The independent study tasks are meant to be followed by you *during* the course, you won't have time to do them all *before* the course! They are intended to allow you to read ahead of your class, which is a great way to ensure that you arrive well prepared for the exams in the summer of year 13. They are intended to encourage you to be organised and to manage your own time. And they are there to provide an extra layer of challenge, to make sure that you are studying at the highest level possible throughout your A Level course, which you'll need to do if you want the highest grades.

This is the section designed to be useful to you throughout the two years you'll be studying A Level Physics, with loads of activities and study ideas to keep you interested. Something in this section of the book will help you when you are feeling the pressure of imminent exams, or when you don't feel like you have the motivation to do another page of calculation questions, or when you got a disappointing grade on a topic test.

The last section of the book is about you as a learner and the habits you'll need to develop to be a success at A Level Physics. There is a chapter detailing some of the fundamental skills for learning Physics and some questions to make sure that you recognise just how much these skills underpin all the content in A Level Physics.

Finally some ideas about study skills and a really important chapter on making sure you are being evaluative about the impact of the particular study activities that you are doing. This is called metacognition and too many A Level students are no good at this! Read it carefully and take it seriously if you want the top grades at A Level.

More About the Challenge of A Level Physics

This book will help you get ready of A Level Physics. Many books that are designed to do this focus on algebra, units, calculations and other core skills in physics. Unfortunately, just doing that type of task won't prepare you for the highest levels of challenge!

At A Level there are far fewer recall questions than at GCSE, and fewer "explain" type questions. In fact just about every question at A Level starts from the applying skill level. They will give you a context, and probably one that you haven't studied before, or they haven't used in exam questions before. You'll find several study tasks which help you understand the challenge posed by A Level questions.

Students realise very early that the way in which they prepared for GCSEs will not help them passing their A Levels. You need to become an expert in problem solving and to do that you need to be fluent in Physics. You need to get good, not just at memorising and understanding content, but at recognising content within unfamiliar contexts and applying your knowledge to solve the problems.

Apply type questions are just the baseline difficulty at A Level. The analytical, evaluative and the creative challenges require deep thinking, under time pressure in the exam. You must train yourself to work at this high level throughout the two years you study the A Level.

Don't be too harsh on yourself if you find A Level Physics hard. Remember that students who get less than a grade 6 in the new GCSEs will probably not go on to study A-level sciences. At A level you are competing with the most able students in your year group across the country. We do not talk about a C grade being a "good pass" at A level! Even an E grade is still a good grade which carries UCAS points and allows you to apply to university.

Introductions to A Level Physics Topics

Congratulations on picking the greatest A Level of all! A Level Physics!

A Level Physics is a real challenge, but it's also a hugely fascinating study. I really hope you enjoy learning Physics. These next few pages are just a quick overview to give you some idea of what you should be looking forward to over the next two years of study.

The more you can see the relevance and the interest of the work you are doing the more you'll enjoy it, and the more you enjoy your study the better you will do at it.

Becoming fluent in Physics requires that you have a good knowledge of all the topic areas and can draw on a broad and accurate knowledge of them all. Every A Level course tests your synoptic ability, that is your ability to combine knowledge and skills from more than one section of the course to solve problems or to synthesise an argument.

It's important to take a wholistic view of the content of your course. Try and build a map of the course in your mind as you learn each topic. Look out for common links between topics and be prepared to think on your feet in exams.

Pro-tip: Get ahead of your class! You don't need to wait to read the textbook or watch YouTube videos at the same pace as the rest of your class or the teacher. Look ahead and be already familiar with the hardest topics when you come to them in lessons. This is the best way to become fluent in Physics.

Mechanics

Mechanics is tricky, at first! There are loads of equations to get your head around. Normally you study mechanics first so it's where you get yourself up to the standards required at A Level. You'll have to handle large amounts of data at once, converting units, and rearranging complex formula.

The first thing to get your head around is all the International System (SI) of units and their prefixes. I always suggest students begin by learning to express each derived unit in terms of their base units. Here are the SI base units and some examples of derived units expressed in base units.

Base Quantity	SI Base Unit	Derived Quantity	SI Derived Unit	Unit Expressed in Base Units
Length	m	Force	N	$kgms^{-2}$
Time	s	Pressure	Pa	$kgm^{-1}s^{-2}$
Current	A	Charge	C	As
Temperature	K	p.d.	V	$kgm^{2}s^{-3}A^{-1}$
Mass	kg	Power	W	$kgm^{2}s^{-3}$

This idea of deriving quantities from few base quantities is the beginning of understanding dimensional analysis. Dimensional analysis is a tool that Physicists use to develop and to check new theories! Really you can understand it as simply as this: *the two sides of an equation have the equivalent units.* You cannot, for example make a watt equal to a volt! Sounds obvious to say, but it is something that needs to be stated. (I have omitted the base units candela and mole as they are not useful to us in A Level Physics.)

Physicists gather in vast conventions to discuss the use of and the values of the SI units. In 1960 Physicists decided upon these five SI quantities and their units and defined their values relative to some measurable standard. For example; the metre is the length of 1 650 763.73 wavelengths of a radiation from krypton-86; a second is 9 192 631 770 periods of a radiation from caesium-133, a kilogram is the mass as of an inert block of alloy, stored in a vacuum called the platinum-iridium prototype!

These five quantities were chosen primarily because we have ways of measuing them directly. For example; we have an instrument to measure distance, usually in the lab a metre rule, and an instrument to measure time, a stopwatch, but we do not have an instrument to measure speed directly. Speed therefore must be calculated, or derived, from distance and time. We can measure current directly using a galvanometer, a type of coiled wire which attracts itself magnetically when a current flows through it, all other electrical meters, (e.g. voltmeters and ohmmeters,) are based on this, and so the quantities are derived. We can measure temperature directly using and thermometer and mass directly using a mass balance, other, less directly measurable quantities are derived from them.

This might seem a little over the top to you to have definitions to such a degree of precision. Think however of the precision this allows experimenters to work to high degrees of precision. If we want to measure universal constants to ten significant figures, well we better have our units defined to at least ten significant figures as well! Subsequent conferences refined these definitions still further to greater and greater resolution. This was all fine until very recently when Physicists started to feel that they were approaching this idea of defining units from the wrong direction.

You see a universal constant is just that, constant everywhere in the universe, so rather than define units in which to measure these constants, lets define the unit by the constant. In May 2019 Physicists agreed to redefine units as related to universal constants! Then as our measurement of these universal constants get more accurate then so does our system of units. The metre is now defined using the speed of light, the Ampere is now defined using the charge on an electron and the kilogram is now defined using the Planck constant. Only the second and the Kelvin have their definition unchanged.

One of the first challenges in mechanics is using the *equations of linear motion*, (or the *suvat* equations as they are commonly called.) These are equations that can be applied to any situation where the acceleration is constant. Look out for clues like *ignore the effects of air resistance*, or *accelerated by a constant resultant force* to indicate that you should use one of these equations.

These are derived from the equations for velocity and acceleration that you should already know from GCSE:

acceleration is the rate of change of velocity, where a is acceleration, v, is the final velocity and u is the initial velocity, t is the time taken for the change

$$a = \frac{v - u}{t} \qquad (1)$$

this can be rearranged for our first *suvat* equation

$$v = u + at \qquad (2)$$

the next *suvat* starts from the equation linking displacement, s, average velocity, $\frac{u+v}{2}$, and time

$$s = \frac{u + v}{2} t \qquad (3)$$

substitute equation (2) into equation (3)

$$s = \frac{u + (u + at)}{2} t \qquad (4)$$

simplification gives

$$s = ut + \frac{1}{2} at^2 \qquad (5)$$

lastly rearrange equation (2) for t

$$t = \frac{v - u}{a} \qquad (6)$$

substitute equation (6) into equation (3)

$$s = \left(\frac{u + v}{2}\right)\left(\frac{v - u}{a}\right) \qquad (7)$$

expand and simplify for the last *suvat* equation

$$v^2 = u^2 + 2as \qquad (8)$$

I hope you followed this derivation, revisit this a few times, as derivation is a core skill for A Level Physics. Using *suvat* is just a matter of knowing which of the quantities you have and selecting an equation with just one unknown.

This is a stroboscopic photo which can be used to calculate the acceleration due to gravity. The flash that you see in the bottom right of the photo was fired at 20Hz, so you are seeing the same ping pong ball 14 times, each 1/20th of a second apart. The object in the clamp is a half metre rule to allow you to scale the photo. How close to the true value of *9.81ms⁻¹* can you get using it?

For me the most interesting application of mechanics is to sports. If you do not become a professional or elite sports person your Physics can still give you access to a career in sports. Sports teams, organisations and equipment manufacturers invest heavily into Physics research to improve performance.

This is a high speed photograph taken in 1880 used to determine whether a horse's hooves all left the ground at once during a gallop! This was just the start of mechanics analysis making a big impact in sports. In the present day computational models are applied to tennis racquet design and the sub two hour marathon was made possible by kinetic energy recovery shoes! Physics is a massive part of sport.

You'll also learn dynamics, which is how forces cause or alter motion. It'll get tricky here as you need to work in two dimensions, including using Pythagoras's theorem and trigonometry. One of the most interesting and satisfying things you'll learn is how objects move under gravity in projectile motion, you'll have to put together all the skills you've developed to solve these difficult problems.

Like anything; practice loads, learn the tricks and you'll do really well!

DC Electricity

Your phone contains billions of electrical switches called transistors which are 7nm in diameter. To put that into context; an atom is in the order of 0.1nm! Miniaturisation is the process of making chipsets and microprocessors smaller and smaller such that higher rates of computation are possible in more portable form factors. *Moore's Law* states simply that the number of transistors in average chipsets doubles every two years, therefore computing power doubles every two years. However we are approaching a limit; transistors of a size less than fifty atoms across will become unreliable, as quantum tunnelling effects begin to occur. It's an often-quoted factoid that your phone has more computing power than took man to the moon; (this milestone was in fact met long ago, before we were even playing snake in 1998 on the Nokia 5110!) Your iPhone has something like 100 000 times the computing power of the Apollo 11 guidance computer. Your standard school calculator has more computing power than *all* of NASA's computers in 1969!

This microscope photograph shows an AMD Ryzen 7nm transistor chip – spot the 8 cores!

Consumers have moved from feature phones, with low powered screens and processors, to smart phones with power hungry OLED panels, multicore processors and dedicated graphics processors. Tech companies have needed to develop power systems to allow users a full day of charge, and battery recharge circuits which are powerful enough to fully charge a phone in one hour. All this needs to fit in a form factor which can fit into your pocket. Physics is your route into this world of design.

Circuit design is an integral part of all appliance design; from communitcations sattelites and robots on their way to Jupiter's moons, to kettles and solar charging battery packs. For many people it will be their most challenging area of Physics, but like all Physics there are a few laws and principles which will set you in good stead to solve technical problems in the future and solve written problems that they will set you in the exams!

Before you start make sure you have a correct definition of *potential difference, current* and *resistance* in your head. If you aren't sure, take the time to revisit electricity at GSCE level!

In Electricity at A Level you are going to come across a lot of new quantities that you didn't meet at GCSE. These three quantities are crucial to understand before you build up your full understanding of electricity. I think a great deal of students find this topic hard because they have never got a useful model of electricity firmly in their mind. They've just muddled through GCSE with good maths skills to solve electricity problems! You need to build new understanding on solid, technically correct ideas, otherwise misconceptions will arise!

The three quantities; *potential difference, V,* (often incorrectly called *voltage*), *current, I,* and *resistance, R,* are linked by Ohm's Law: potential difference is proportional to current, and the gradient of a V vs I graph is the resistance. (It is more useful to plot V on the y-axis so that the gradient is directly R.)

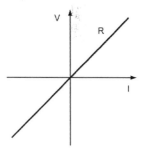

$$potential\ difference = current \times resistance$$

$$V = IR$$

Here are their definitions:

Potential difference - The difference in energy per unit charge between two points in a circuit.

Current - The rate of flow of charge.

Resistance - A measure of a component's opposition to flow of charge.

Did any of those definitions surprise you? If they did, take your time, go back and look at the GCSE section on electricity or look again at the models of electricity that you studied as far back as when you were twelve or thirteen years old!

The same can be said about Kirchhoff's Laws. Kirchhoff's Laws are just the relationship between potential differences and currents in series and parallel circuits from your GCSE. We use them to work out unknown values in circuits. Together with Ohm's Law they provide a toolkit for solving all circuit problems.

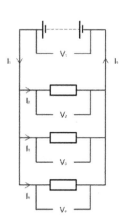

You need to be able to calculate quantities in tricky looking circuits accurately if you are going to be a success in this section of the A Level curriculum.

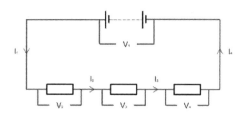

Pro-tip: You can often define quantities using their equations. Look back at the definitions of current, potential difference and resistance and notice that the words describe the relationship expressed in these three equations.

$$I = \frac{\Delta Q}{t} \qquad V = \frac{E}{Q} \qquad R = \frac{V}{I}$$

Materials

How do you lay the foundations for a building that twists as it rises into the sky? What materials do you choose so that it's light enough but tough enough to resist the torsional (twisting) forces involved? In materials you'll learn the fundamentals of the science behind engineering on the largest scales and the smallest scales.

Have you ever considered a career in sweet design? Confectioners employ physicists to achieve the chewy or brittle consistencies for their sweets.

Can you see the link between the design of a twisted marshmallow and a twisted building?

I really enjoy teaching this topic, there are some great experiments and interesting contexts that you can apply your knowledge to.

If you are interested in engineering this is the topic for you. Hooke's Law graphs and Young Modulus graphs will test and improve your ideas about proportionality.

You'll investigate flow rates, viscosity and terminal velocity. From this you'll get the idea of dimensional analysis. Skip forward to task 3 if you want to know right away how to measure and compare viscosities of various kitchen fluids.

Pro-tip: Materials seems on the face of it like a straightforward topic. But learn definitions and concepts in this topic well, because they often come up as synoptic links in other areas. For example, stiffness (the gradient of a force-extension graph) is used in waves and oscillations topics.

Waves

Waves and oscillations are fascinating! Every time I revisit it my understanding of it changes and improves. In fact, of all things in Physics waves and oscillations have the most far reaching applications. Especially if you are interested in continuing in Physics beyond A Level you will find the understanding of waves to be crucial, and you need to be secure with this topic before we get into wave-particle duality in quantum.

Before you start, make sure you have a good working knowledge of all the basic wave quantities and wave behaviours. Early in this topic you will go on to tackle new ideas of Huygens's construction, standing waves and interference.

You'll also discover how a simple wave form is related to trigonometry, using sine and cosine function graphs to draw wave forms accurately. So that means that triangles, circles and waves are all inextricably linked! Amazing.

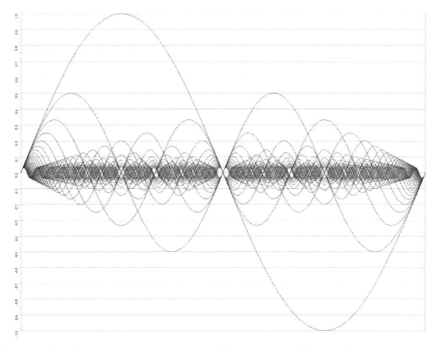

Waves explain how we communicate and how we see. They explain earthquakes and our understanding of the structure of the Earth. They let us explore our universe and how we can make and appreciate music. They let us cook and scan for lung infections or do pre-natal scans. We can use them for echo location and to explain how two light rays can meet and produce darkness! Without knowledge of waves we wouldn't be far out of the dark ages!

During the renaissance new knowledge of waves was applied to music. Theories of harmonics replaced trial and error in instrument design. Before this instruments were designed by plucking at lengths of string to find the most pleasing sounds. Suddenly, using this maths, new shapes of instruments which amplified the right notes and left the other vibrations supressed. Elegant designs of harps, violins, clarinets and the piano replaced lutes, horns and bells.

A harmonic series of waves, like the one in the diagram, is a set of waves with frequencies in even multiples of a fundamental frequency. You'll investigate this using Melde's Apparatus, by making standing waves on a string. Harmony is the foundation of all music, and waves are the foundation of a great deal of Physics!

Pro-tip: learn these definitions by heart:
Wave speed - the distance a wave travels every second.
Frequency - the number of waves per second.
Wavelength - the distance from a point on a wave to the same point on the next wave.
Time Period - the time taken for one full wave cycle.
Amplitude - the height of a wave from its centre line (equilibrium position.)

... and make sure you know good explanations of the three wave behaviours:
Reflection - waves change direction at opaque boundaries with angles of incidence equal to angle of reflection
Refraction - waves change direction as they speed up or slow down at an interface between mediums, the ratio of sine of the angle of incidence to the sine of the angle of reflection is a constant for each interface known as the refractive index.
Diffraction - when waves travel through a gap approximately equal to their wavelength they spread out into semi-circular patterns.
Interference - when two coherent waves meet they superpose; a new wave is created with displacement equal to the sum of the two displacements which created it.
Only waves show these four behaviours. If you can show something does all of these behaviours, it is a wave!

Quantum

You'll probably start this topic learning about one of the most important debates in the history of Physics; the nature of light. *Is light a wave or a Particle?*

Task 6 will help you go into this in more detail but, briefly, the debate goes something like this: Isaac Newton thought light is a particle, he called it a *corpuscle*, science was happy with this explanation for some time, after all Sir Isaac Newton was a pretty smart dude! This model was limited though, and scientists knew there were things that it couldn't explain.

Thomas Young, (the same that defined the *Young Modulus* from the materials chapter), changed things two hundred years after Newton. His double slit experiment shows that light can interfere! Amazingly, (as this is a wave behaviour...) surely light must be a wave.

In the early twentieth century Hertz and Planck were looking at a phenomenon that couldn't be explained using wave theory. This is the photoelectric effect!

The photoelectric effect is the emission of electrons from metal surfaces due to light. The light energy was being transferred to the electrons giving them enough energy to escape the atom. Nothing surprising so far, except that *only* light above a certain frequency showed this effect.

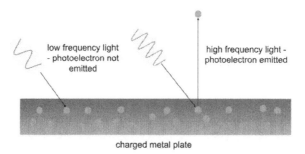

low frequency light - photoelectron not emitted

high frequency light - photoelectron emitted

charged metal plate

It puzzled them! The problem was that waves are continuous, so should transfer their energy continuously. Low frequency light should just take longer time or higher intensity to transfer enough energy to the electrons to release them from their atoms. This wasn't seen! For this reason, it was clear that the wave model of light was limited.

In 1905 Albert Einstein solved the problem; he gave us Einstein's photoelectric equation. Light must be both, a wave and a particle! We call a wave-particle of light a photon, it has an energy equal to its frequency, f, multiplied by the Planck constant h. The work function, φ, is the minimum energy required to release a photoelectron. This is all calculated by measuring the energies of the highest speed electrons emitted.

energy of a photon = work function + maximum kinetic energy of photoelectron

$$hf = \varphi + \frac{1}{2}mv_{max}^2$$

The equation essentially shows that one photon interacts with one electron. Some of the photon energy, hf, is used raising the electron up from its energy level within the atom, *the work function,* and the rest is given to the electron as kinetic energy. It shows us the discrete energy levels within the atoms, and that other observed phenomena such as absorption spectra from stars, or emission spectrums from Florescent lights can be explained by electrons moving up or down the energy levels, with energy changes corresponding to fixed *quanta* of energy.

Quantum is your first excursion into Einsteinian physics, enjoy it! Be aware that it can get very tricky at times, so take your time, and take Richard Feynman's advice "If you want to understand quantum mechanics, just do the math. All the words that are spun around it don't mean very much." That's solid advice for most of Physics to be honest!

Quantum mechanics is the most successful model of the 20th Century, after the quantisation of light into the photon model, experiments followed which showed the same quantisation was possible for almost every part of nature! This seemed the most likely route to an eventual *theory of everything,* a grand unifying theory which could explain one and everything in a single coherent set of rules. In fact everything was quantizable, everything except gravity.

In 1909 Robert Millikan showed that the electronic charge, e, was a discrete unit of charge. You'll read about this when you come across his oil drop experiment, where he essentially held charge oil drops in a electrical field and showed that the charge on them was always a multiple of $1.6 \times 10^{-19}C$. This number will come up time and time again. It's that relative charge that you are probably familiar with, i.e. that an electron has a charge of -1, a proton has a charge of +1, and alpha particle +2, and so on. These are all just multiples of $1.6 \times 10^{-19} C$.

Perhaps the most surprising finding of quantum physics though is that wave-particle duality was not limited to light. Louis de Broglie, (pronounced *de Broy*,) received the 1929 Nobel Prize for his hypothesis that in fact all particles, all matter, can be thought of as having both wave and particle properties. Essentially, depending on the situation, they would show wave behaviour or particle behaviour. Experiment after experiment showed that particles could be *diffracted,* an exclusively wave behaviour, and they behaved like waves with a wavelength which could be predicted based on their momentum by his equation, which included the same universal constant, the Planck constant, *h*.

$$\lambda = \frac{h}{p} \qquad de\ Broglie\ wavelength = \frac{Planck\ constant}{momentum}$$

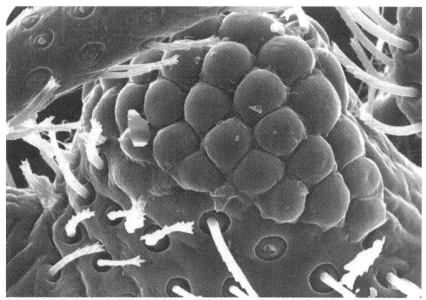

Electrons would be diffracted most with a gap size closest to their de Broglie wavelength. This can be used to build up images with astonishing resolution, which would never be possible with light microscopes.

The Transmission Electron Microscope, TEM, which analyses the diffraction patterns of electrons as they diffract and then interfere with one another after passing through the tiniest of gaps, such as the structures of this eye of a bed-bug in the image above.

Further Mechanics

This topic contains higher demand mechanics concepts and ones which you'll need to apply to some of the other second year physics topics. It is therefore common for examiners to bring in further mechanics concepts into synoptic questions, so make sure you are fluent with them.

In this section you'll meet conservation of momentum in two dimensions. I think this is one of the most demanding areas of physics mathematically. Really though it's not much more complicated than working with any vector in two dimensions, but it does throw up some counter intuitive answers, so you need to trust your maths!

Conservation of momentum at GCSE was only ever in one dimension, meaning that the momentum before a collision is always equal to the momentum after a collision. This can allow us to work out velocities of objects after collisions, based on knowing their masses and their velocities before a collision. This can be generalised to all situations involving two objects colliding. Where m is the mass, u is the initial velocity and v is the final velocity:

$$m_1 u_1 + m_2 u_2 = m_1 v_1 + m_2 v_2$$

Generalising this into two dimensions is just the same as working with vectors in two dimensions. You need to resolve each vector into x and y components. Make this simple for yourself and always work with angles between the velocities and the horizontal, that way you are always using the cosine trig function for all the x components, and you are always using sine for the y components.

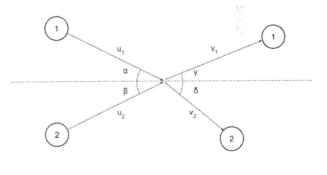

x dimension:	$m_1 u_1 cos\alpha + m_2 u_2 cos\beta = m_1 v_1 cos\gamma + m_2 v_2 cos\delta$
y dimension:	$m_1 u_1 sin\alpha + m_2 u_2 sin\beta = m_1 v_1 sin\gamma + m_2 v_2 sin\delta$

Insert all the values you are given, including those you know are zero, into these equations and you can solve any momentum in two dimensions question. Watch out for the tricky ones where it seems like you have too many unknowns to solve the situation, but these can be solved by treating them as simultaneous equations or sometimes by applying your trig laws, and the identity that:

$$\tan \theta = \frac{\sin \theta}{\cos \theta}$$

Conservation of momentum is used to analyse road traffic accidents. After a crash, forensic scientists can analyse the patterns of debris, skid marks and positions of the damaged vehicles and work back to the conditions under which the collision occurred. They can tell if one, or both, of the cars were speeding. There is no hiding from this, as conservation of momentum is a physical law, and physical laws cannot be broken!

This branch of Physics is also applied during the extensive road safety tests that cars go through before being sold.

In further mechanics you will also meet circular motion. Circular motion is a useful area of physics which ties together topics of Simple Harmonic Motion, Particle Physics and Astrophysics. The equations for motion in a circle are some of the most often used in synoptic questions, the most challenging questions at A Level. Circular motion is defined by the equation for a centripetal force. It is this resultant force towards the centre of a circle which causes this constant acceleration towards the centre, remembering that an acceleration is a rate of change of speed or direction.

$$F = \frac{mv^2}{r}$$

Where F is the centripetal force, m is the mass of the object, v its speed and r is the radius of the circle. Isaac Newton came up with a useful analogy for explaining motion in a circle. If you were to fire a cannon ball horizontally at just the right speed it would make one complete orbit of the Earth and hit you in the back of the head. Too fast and it would climb away from Earth, too slow and it would spiral down to Earth. (This is all of course ignoring the effects of air resistance or other terrestrial objects interacting with it.) This turns out to be a model which fits exactly to the orbits of satellites and is explained by the equation above, the force being provide by the object's weight.

Common demonstrations of circular motion lead to misconceptions. For example; whirl a bucket full of water on a string and the water does not fall out, drive a car fast around a corner and you feel that you are being pushed to the outside of the car. You'll be forgiven for saying, *there must be a force pushing you outwards from the centre of the circle.* Sounds logical but apply a bit of reasoned thinking and experimenting and you'll soon discover that the force keeping an object moving in a circle must be towards the centre of that circle.

Whirl an object on a string around your head and ask yourself what force you are doing on it to keep it spinning. You must be pulling on the string. So, what of that *feeling* of being pushed to the outside of the car, that does happen. Let's call it the centrifugal effect. It's an effect of inertia. At any instant the object is moving with a speed and direction, without a resultant force it will keep doing that its speed and direction will remain unchanged, it will keep going in a straight line. The feeling of being pushed to the outside of the car is actually because your body wants to keep going straight on, so the car is actually pushing on you, to accelerate you in a circle!

You can show this principle by whirling an object on a string above your head, let go and you remove the force. It will keep on moving in the direction it was going at that instant.

Simple Harmonic Motion

This topic builds upon the first-year topic of waves. In fact, waves are an example of a simple harmonic oscillation (SHM).

It's important that you have a good definition of SHM so that you can recognise the contexts that they give you where you can apply the equations and other details you will learn in this topic.

A simple harmonic motion is an oscillation around a point, where there is a force *towards* that point which is *proportional to the object's displacement* from that point. That sounds like quite a lot, but it's not really complicated at all, in fact it can all be summed up in the equation $F = -k\Delta x$, (Hooke's Law but with an important minus sign!)

There are some interesting applications and contexts for SHM! It is a topic which is a fascinating study, but first get your head around the sine function graphs below and keep coming back to them whenever the questions get tricky. Later on, in this book you can get started with exploring this amazing topic by analysing the motion of a pendulum.

If you already know a little about trigonometry then you will probably recognise these three graphs as a cosine graph, a negative sine graph and a negative cosine graph. These are all related to each other by calculus, just as any set of motion graphs are. All SHM follows these graphs and these graphs all follow from the definition of SHM that I gave you above, $F = -k\Delta x$.

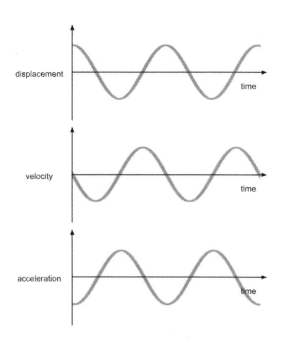

Particle Physics

I love teaching this topic, because it's where so many of the answers to the puzzles of our Universe lie. Amazingly the answers to the largest questions about our universe lie at the smallest scale.

You may have heard it said that scientists at the Large Hadron Collider, (the LHC at CERN,) are trying to recreate the conditions just after the big bang. What they are talking about is *trying to answer to the most fundamental questions at the fundamental scale.*

For example, the LHCb experiment is trying to solve the puzzle of why we are living in a matter universe. Theoretically every time we create matter, we should also create an equal amount of antimatter, and the two should've annihilated one another immediately... and well... nothing should ever have happened. The hypothesis is that, unlike all other known particles, when b particles are made there is a slightly higher incidence of matter b particles than anti-matter b particles are made. If that hypothesis were supported, then these b particles, (sometimes called *beauty* or *bottom* particles, you decide which name you want to use) are the probable answer to one of the Universe's fundamental questions, *why are we made of matter?*

This image was the first empirical evidence for the existence of antimatter. The evidence finally explained an interesting second solution to some equations that Paul Dirac wrote to encompass all known particles *within* the theories of special relativity and quantum mechanics. He suggested no reason for

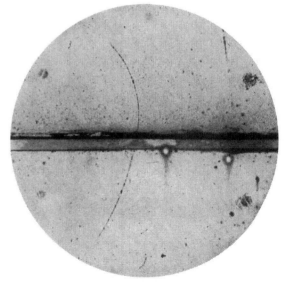

the second solution, but this mathematical anomaly was revisited when Carl Anderson took this photograph in 1930. It shows the tracks of a charged particle as it smashes through a metal plate. It's travelling upwards as we look at it, you can tell because it has less momentum and so curves more after it has collided with the plate. It has the same radius of curvature as an electron, but it curves the *wrong* way in the magnetic field! It is the same as an electron, but positive, it is an antimatter electron, a *positron*!

The search for the fundamental captivated me when I was a student, and now I love teaching it. You'll discover the Standard Model, (which is like our periodic table for Physics,) our latest and best model to explain how fundamental particles. You'll learn the four fundamental forces; gravitational, electromagnetic, strong nuclear and weak nuclear, and the particles which we call bosons, which carry them; the graviton, the photon, the gluon, and the W and Z bosons.

You'll discover how the energy frontiers, quantum boundaries were broken, how our conception of the fundamental has changed over time, as you learn the principles behind particle acceleration and detection.

You'll learn a lot of the satisfying rules, patterns and symmetries that govern this 10^{-15}m universe, and how matter and antimatter are created and are annihilated. Particle Physics is the type of topic that seems complicated at first but in fact has some straightforward principles which if you learn well will help you solve any problem they can throw at you.

Pro-tip: memorise the Standard Model, Q represents the charge on the particle.

Fermions		1st Generation	2nd Generation	3rd Generation	Bosons
Quarks	Q	$+\dfrac{2}{3}$ up	$+\dfrac{2}{3}$ charm	$+\dfrac{2}{3}$ top	gluon
	Q	$-\dfrac{1}{3}$ down	$-\dfrac{1}{3}$ strange	$-\dfrac{1}{3}$ bottom	photon
Leptons	Q	-1 electron	-1 muon	-1 tau	W^- & W^+
	Q	0 electron-neutrino	0 muon-neutrino	0 tau-neutrino	Z^0

Briefly, Quarks go together to make baryons (groups of three quarks,) and mesons (quark anti-quark pairs,) leptons are fundamental. Bosons carry the fundamental forces, strong nuclear, electromagnetic and weak nuclear respectively.

Electromagnetism

Electric and magnetic fields are inextricably linked. In fact, as you will learn in your particle physics topic they are carried by the same fundamental force; the electromagnetic force and its exchange boson, the photon.

There are some crucial rules and laws that you will learn about how the two fields behave and interact. This crucial understanding will explain how generators, motors and transformers work. You'll need to be fluent in applying Coulomb's Law and Faraday's Law of electromagnetic induction, as well as able to explain how a Hall probe works and able to investigate magnetic flux. You can study Coulomb's law in independent task 11.

They are examples of Force Fields, the maths gets quite complicated at times, but think of it in terms of what would happen if you were to put a particle in the field. *What forces would be exerted on it?* This will help you understand the ideas of *field strengths*, *potentials* and *energies*.

Lastly we analyse the capacitor, which is a device which stores charge by setting up an electrical field. We use exponentials to define the trends by which they charge and discharge. This will likely be the first time you have come across exponential equations in Physics, it is a huge synoptic element in A Level Physics and you need to make sure it is a skill you can do easily.

Pro-tip: Fields are tricky to get your head around, especially it is easy to get muddled in definitions like potential. *Always therefore start your definitions from ideas you do understand, link electrical potential to the idea of a potential difference, and recognise that a potential is only one quantity away from being an electrical potential energy. Concepts like this often make sense if you think about their units. An electrical potential has units JC^{-1} (joules per coulomb,) multiply that by charge, you have a joule, i.e. energy. Similarly, with electrical field strength, this is defined as a force per unit charge, it has units NC^{-1}, multiply field strength by charge and you have a Newton, i.e. a force. This type of reasoning can be applied to every type of field you study; work through the algebra that's where your understanding will come from.*

Nuclear Physics

I can't wait to start teaching Nuclear Physics at any level! It's amazing once students start to picture the nucleus as dynamic and unstable and understand that vast values of energy are released in nuclear reactions.

In this topic you will use Einstein's famous $E = mc^2$ equation to calculate just how much energy is released from a small change in mass! Einstein's involvement in the Manhattan project, the group of scientists who worked on the Physics to make the atomic bomb a reality, haunted him for the rest of his life. He famously stated "if only I had known, I would've become a watchmaker. This image shows the *Trinity Test* which was the first ever detonation of a nuclear device.

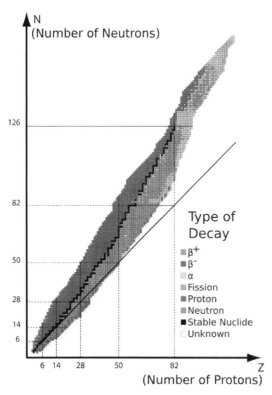

There are nuclear equations to contend with which are perhaps some of the simplest elements of the A Level course, but then there are conceptually challenging graphs which explain nuclear stability, nuclear binding energy, alpha, beta and gamma decay, fission and fusion.

This graph shows all of the currently known isotopes. The black points are stable isotopes, those above this roughly described trend decay by beta minus, those below by beta plus. The heavier and manmade elements tend to decay by alpha, or even fission.

Nuclear stability is not a simple binary situation though, it is a continuum, with isotopes being more, or less, stable. In fact every isotope has a definite probability of decaying, this is where we get the idea of radioactive emissions being random, and it follows from that random nature that we can only describe the decay of a group of particles by finding the fixed times for fixed ratios of change. For example, the *half-life* of an isotope is the average time taken for the number of nuclei or the activity to decay by half. You can study this more in the 3rd experiment in the *Try This at Home* section of the book.

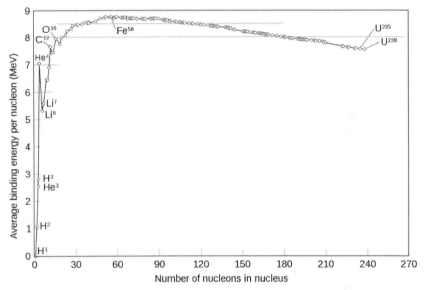

This graph also plots many isotopes to reveal a reason why there is a difference in the stability of radioisotopes. It plots their average binding energy per nucleon vs their nucleon number. Notice that Iron-56 is the peak of the graph, it is the most stable isotope. It requires the most energy to separate a nucleon from the nucleus. Notice some other extraordinarily stable isotopes, which are above the general trend, Helium-4, Carbon-12 and Oxygen-16 are all very stable arrangements of nucleons. It also follows that the elements that are lighter than iron release energy when they are formed in nuclear fusion, and elements heavier than iron require energy to be made by fusion. This is just one of the many synoptic elements in explaining how stars are formed and what happens at the end of their stellar evolutions.

Gravitational Fields

Isaac Newton didn't discover gravity, what he realised was that the same force which caused the apple to fall on his head which also caused the Earth to revolve around the Sun and the Moon to revolve around the Earth. He used Kepler's laws to derive his Law of Universal Gravitation; *the force is proportional to the product of the two masses over the radius squared.*

Later Henry Cavendish was able to establish the constant of proportionality for this law with a gigantic experiment, involving huge lead masses rotating relative to even bigger fixed masses. We call this constant G, the Universal Gravitational Constant.

There are just a few puzzling differences between gravitational field and electric or magnetic fields, for example gravity is always attractive! Gravity acts upon mass, and you cannot have negative mass like you can have negative charge or opposite poles of a magnet. In fact these differences are just a few of the unexplained elements of our current best theories of everything, *the Standard Model* and *Einstein's Theory of General Relativity*. Many experiments give strong evidence for these two explanations, but we have yet to find a mechanism for gravity, and that is a major stumbling block in our search to explain the Universe around us.

This is a fascinating topic, but make sure you can apply the maths fluently because it comes into synoptic questions quite a lot, for example considering gravitational forces as centripetal forces in satellite orbits.

Pro-tip: Understanding one type of field will help you understand another. Here's a table comparing some quantities in gravitational and electrical fields.

Quantity	Gravity Fields		Electric Fields	
field strength	$g = \dfrac{F}{m}$	$g = \dfrac{-Gm_1}{r^2}$	$E = \dfrac{F}{Q} = \dfrac{V}{d}$	$E = k\dfrac{Q_1}{r^2}$
force	$F = \dfrac{-Gm_1 m_2}{r^2}$		$F = k\dfrac{Q_1 Q_2}{r^2}$	
potential	$V_g = \dfrac{-Gm_1}{r}$		$V = k\dfrac{Q_1}{r}$	
potential energy	$E = \dfrac{-Gm_1 m_2}{r}$	$E = mgh$	$E = k\dfrac{Q_1 Q_2}{r}$	$E = QV$

Thermal Physics

Thermal Physics gets a bit of a bad rap with teachers and students alike. I'm a bit sick of hearing "Thermodynamics... uggghhhh!" Thermodynamics is the science of how heat moves, and it can explain so much of the Universe, not to mention being incredibly useful.

Thermodynamic differences are the drivers of change, in fact without these energy differences, nothing would happen. The phrase *the inevitable heat death of the Universe* is a common presumption of the eventual fate of everything, which is that everything tends towards thermal equilibrium. That is a compelling hypothesis and works if we presume a closed system. Recent measurements show though that there does seem to be some source of energy driving the change in our Universe and so things do not seem to be tending towards a flat, stationary, stable Universe, but one that is accelerating, with seemingly no limit to its rate of expansion. Whether the driver of this change is energy, or its elusive counterpart dark-energy, the laws of Thermodynamics must surely apply.

The best bit about Thermal Physics though is the experiments that you can do. From these, which you can do accurately in school labs you get the three gas laws.

The first should be most familiar to you, Boyle's Law, *for a fixed mass of gas at a constant temperature, pressure is inversely proportional to volume.*

$$p \propto \frac{1}{V}$$

You can get pretty good approximation of the second gas law, Charles' law, just with a balloon and a few hot or cold places around your home. I'm sure you can figure out a way to accurately measure the circumference of a balloon and then calculate the volume of a balloon from that. You can estimate the temperatures of the fridge or a freezer, room temperature, and maybe submerged in a sink of warm water or above a radiator.

Charles' Law, states that *for a fixed mass of gas at a constant pressure, the volume is proportional to the temperature.*

$$p \propto V$$

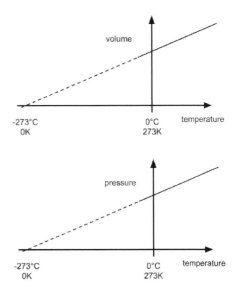

The third gas law, the Gay-Lussac law follows a similar trend, *for a fixed mass of gas at a constant volume, the pressure is proportional to temperature.*

The exiting thing about these two proportional laws is that proportional relationships imply that the trend starts from the origin. That origin is not zero degrees Celsius however. Take the experimental data in the ranges of temperatures you'll be able to measure in the lab and extrapolate back to the point where a gas would occupy zero volume o be at zero pressure. That point would be absolute zero; zero degrees kelvin or -273 degrees Celsius. The coldest anything can theoretically be.

The three gas laws combine into the ideal gas equation:

$$pV = NkT$$

where N is the number of molecules of gas and k is the Boltzmann constant.

Without the study of thermodynamics there would never have been steam engines, nor motor cars, and forget keeping your drink cold in the fridge... what a sad world it would be indeed. Thermodynamics may allow us to account for the Universe being here at all! It may be the reason life exists at all, that we are just a convenient mechanism for speeding up the dissipation of energy... fascinating!

If you can't get excited about that then you may have picked the wrong A Level!

Astrophysics

Space exploration presents a lot of problems. We, as humans, haven't gone very far really... I mean the moon is far, but it's just around the corner when compared to other astronomical distances. Even at the speed of light it would take eight minutes to get to the sun, or four years to our next nearest star. For this reason, most of space physics is about how we take measurements of our Universe without actually going to these places.

For example, we use *trigonometric parallax* to measure distances to nearby stars. You can probably take a good stab at the meaning of that as you'll have come across both words before in your studies. But try holding your pen out in front of you and closing one eye then the other, the pen seems to move relative to the "fixed" background of the wall, measure the angle between these *parallax* images and the distance between your two eyes, and you can calculate the distance to the pen by trigonometry.

We use standard candles for more distant stars. We analyse the light that comes from these stars and from that we can make conclusions about the temperature and mass of these stars. We can fit them to the trend of *main sequence* stars that we have identified and take a pretty good stab that their luminosity, their power output. Once we know this, we can measure the intensity of their light here on earth and fit this to an inverse square relationship and so calculate their distance.

For even more distant objects we can use variable stars or supernovae to get an accurate estimation of distances. For other galaxies we can use their angular diameter to get an idea of their sizes and the distance to them. Independent task 9 will show you the principle of using angular diameters to measure distances in space.

We are also searching for exoplanets, that is planets that are in other solar systems. We look for evidence in the variation of measured light intensity and make conclusions on what might have passed in front of the star. We can get an idea of the temperature of the planets around distant stars, hence we can see if there are likely to be any planets in that exclusive *Goldilocks* zone; not too hot, not too cold, for liquid water, and therefore life!

The most interesting part of the Astrophysics topic, for me at least is the process of stellar evolution. We can plot a star's journey from nebula to white-dwarf on what we call a Hertzsprung-Russell diagram. An amazing graph.

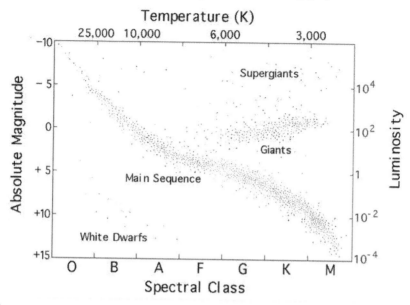

Take a moment to get your head around it. Luminosity is on the y-axis, relative to the brightness of our sun, so the stars at the top of the graph radiate the most light. Temperature is the wrong way around on the x-axis, so the hottest ones are furthest to the left. Temperature is measured by analysing the spectra of the stars and finding their measured by peak wavelength, that is the wavelength which they emit the most of. There are also on this diagram the classes of the stars, and the absolute magnitude of them, but you need not worry about these at A Level. Both the x and y axes are logarithmic axes, meaning that the values do not increase linearly, this is the only way to fit stars with such huge differences in scale on one plot. Think of a log scale as instead of counting *1, 2, 3,* we count *10^1, 10^2, 10^3* and so on.

Our Sun sits right in the middle. A decidedly average star. It sits on the main sequence, the group of stars that are in the stable period of their life cycle, their evolution, during which the outwards forces of radiation pressure and the inwards forces of gravity are balanced. You can see a clear trend between luminosity and temperature for main sequence stars.

Our Sun has been a main sequence star for some four or five billion years and will stay stable for another similar length of time. The brighter-hotter stars to the top left of the sequence, have much shorter lifecycles and will be those that are likely to explode in supernovae. The lower brightness cooler stars are bottom right and have the longest periods.

After the main sequence stars expand and cool, the region of stars in the upper right quadrant of the graph are these red-giants, (the lower group,) and red-supergiant stars, (the highest group.) After the red-giant phase the material that makes up our sun will drift out into space and leave behind a planetary nebula with a white-dwarf at its centre. Eventually that star will cool, and no more fusion will occur, it will be a black dwarf. Or at least we think, because the Universe is not old enough to contain any!

In this topic at A Level you will need to add a lot more detail to your understanding of the processes in stars from your GCSE Physics. This topic brings together so many other topics and so is a common synoptic context. For example your knowledge of nuclear and particle physics will be used to explain why elements heavier than iron have to be made during supernovae and how neutron stars can be left behind. Also you will start to wonder at how gravity works and how it can possibly be so strong that not even light can escape when the most massive supernovae result in black holes.

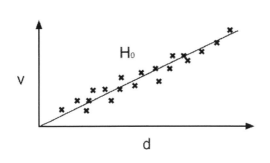

The most significant question in Physics is *when and how did it all begin?* We have a good theory for the beginning, (prepare in A Level to analyse Hubble's data rather than simply quoting his findings!)

Hubble analysed the red-shift of distant galaxies and plotted a graph of recessional velocity, v, against distance from earth, d, whose gradient is inverse the age of the Universe. We call this gradient the Hubble constant or H_0. It has been refined experimentally and we are currently thinking the Universe is about 14 billion years old.

The question *where, when and how will it all end?* Is a little more current in Physics. Our best hypotheses have changed since I studied A Level Physics! *Is the universe, open, closed, flat? Will it expand forever or come back together in a kind of "big crunch"?* The latest evidence shows that it is none of the above, but that it is accelerating! It is expanding, yes, it will go on expanding, yes, but it is expanding at an accelerating rate. This is some of the evidence for the existence of a dark energy, and dark matter; stuff that we cannot see as it seems not to interact with light at all. And this stuff, which we cannot see, which doesn't seem to interact with anything at all and which we know nothing about at all, comprises about 95% of the Universe.

And this is where we are at with Physics today; we know a lot! We have a huge number of Laws, theories and models which explain much of what we see and can do. But this knowledge is only about 5% of the story. Only about 5% of what there is to know. I hope very much that you want to be a part of that story of discovery.

Pro-tip: Whenever you find it hard during your A Levels come back to why you picked them in the first place. Remind yourself of the things that you find fascinating, and this should give you the motivation. Astrophysics is amazing, it's a wonderful topic to study, but without knowledge of thermodynamics, of Newton's Laws and of particle physics you'd be lost trying to understand it! There's a reason to be fascinated by every part of the A Level, every example, every law, every equation has been picked because it is important in its own right. Find cutting edge science articles, watch a few videos about recent experiments and re-kindle your enthusiasm for Physics. That's the best way to get yourself through the hard evenings of study ahead!

Practical Physics

Experiments are important for the practical endorsement and for the exams! But they are so much more than that, they are the Physics. Physics is a science and science is the process of furthering knowledge by experiment. In my experience many capable Physics students do themselves a massive disservice by acting like they aren't interested in conducting the experiments. Students who take Physics tend to be capable mathematicians and tend to enjoy working through calculations. There's something satisfying about a problem which has a definite answer, being able to get to it accurately is the core skill in A Level Physics. But Universities tell us that students get to degree level often incapable of using basic lab equipment or knowing the basic elements of a lab report. There is a particular skill to solving the types of problems that experiments throw-up, and this practical skill takes time and effort to develop.

Core Practicals, PAGs, Required Practicals, Assessed Experiments, whatever your exam board calls them, these experiments are really important parts of these current A Levels. You need to know them inside out!

Your school ~~should~~ must give you the opportunity to conduct them, covering the full range of apparatus and techniques set out in the specification, and they should be keeping a record of all the lab reports that you do for them. To gain a practical endorsement you essentially need to show that you have completed a list of practical skills, don't worry about this, because if you complete all the required experiments you will certainly cover all the skills!

But for the exam, which many of you will be more concerned about, you need to be able to describe each practical in a good level of detail. There will be questions asking you to do just that. You'll also need to be familiar with the techniques, equipment, analysis and methodologies used, and *apply* them to new practicals. You need to be able to plan new experiments yourself under exam conditions.

The best way to do this is to look at the sheets for each experiment that the exam boards have produced. They contain a good indication of the knowledge you need to memorise for the exam from each practical. For example in Edexcel there are a set of questions and answers, which pretty much will be the answers that the exam questions will be driving at. In OCR there is a little note at the end of each PAG sheet explaining which details will be beneficial to know for exams. Don't overlook this stuff when it comes to revision.

I'm going to give you a little mnemonic to remember for these practical questions in exams. It is important that you learn experimentation in sufficient detail to do well in these parts of the exam. It uses the first letter of each syllable of the word experiment… ExPerIMent. This is the thought process that you should go through whenever answering a *describe* or *design* a practical question.

E - Equations. Each experiment starts from an equation, some quantities are measured, some are constant. Think about all the quantities in the equations relevant to the experiment. Make sure you state how to measure or how to control each one, giving values where appropriate.

P - Procedures. Think about what you will do, and how that will improve the accuracy, repeatability, precision or validity of your result. Be detailed, do not just say "measure the…", say what it will be measured with and how, and why this technique will improve the quality of the results.

I - Improvements. No experiment is perfect, no reading is the true value, so *what could be improved?* As you are learning the experiments think evaluatively, what is the best way to do something, what makes one method or piece of apparatus good enough. Evaluation is one of the hardest skills in the A Level, so you need to be good at thinking in this way.

M - Maths. *How are you going to analyse your results? What mathematical models are you going to apply in your experiment? Which graph are you going to plot, and what data does it show?* We like to get our equations resolved so we can plot a straight line, i.e. a $y = mx + c$ graph, ideally with our target data as the gradient. This section may also include the statistics work that you will need to be doing; e.g. means, uncertainties, error bar and lines of most and least slope.

Check out independent tasks 5 and 18 to help you structure your practical revision.

Pro-tip: Exam questions around experiments are really specific. Don't just start writing every detail you know about that practical, decode the question thoroughly and write about exactly what they've asked you about!

Three "Try This at Home" Experiments

Get Excited!

This is a time in your life where you start to specialise, where you start to become a different type of thinker to your friends, where you will find that you know lots about stuff that they know very little, and where you'll start to define how your academic and then professional life is going to be very different to theirs.

Enjoy your studies, enjoy Physics, enjoy turning up each day ready to discover something, to accurately measure something, to prove a rule, to develop a theory you have about something and to add to the evidence that we have about the nature of the universe. Spend this summer getting excited about studying Physics, watch YouTube channels, read books, blogs and magazines, look at universities and find out what research they are doing! Get excited.

These three experiments are designed to give you a low-pressure taste of what experiments in A Level Physics are like. Take them as far as you can, refine them and develop them, but above all, have fun! They are all low risk, but always do a risk assessment, especially if you decide to alter the method in any way. Once you start thinking as an experimenter you'll be amazed at how many things you can measure accurately with just stuff lying around the house!

Each of these three experiments have a detailed method, followed by some analysis and theory questions. I have also included some model answers but make sure you attempt the questions before you look at the answers! Do feel free to stop by GorillaPhysics on YouTube and let me know how they go!

1. Video Analysis

One significant challenge that you will encounter early on in A Level Physics is measuring very small values of time precisely. You'll probably have noticed that whenever we try and do motion practicals with a stopwatch we get huge ranges between repeated results. This is due to our human reaction time, and it is a random error. Repeated measurements can reduce the effects of random error, but with these small increments of time it is best that we remove the human altogether and find some more accurate technique to measure the time.

We use this range as an indication of how uncertain we are of our measurement. We can calculate a value for this uncertainty and use it as a quantitative indication of the quality of our results. It helps us to plan improvements to practicals. For instance; if the largest uncertainty is in timing, it will be worth making a different practical solution for that measurement, or if the largest uncertainty were in measuring distance, we should try and improve our method for measuring that. We estimate uncertainties before collecting results using half a scale division, and we verify our uncertainty as half the range when we have repeated readings.

A common way to reduce uncertainty in timing is to use light gates and data loggers, they have fine resolutions but are not appropriate for all situations, for example when we want to time the motion of something which won't fit through the gate, or we cannot guide it through the beam! In this practical you are going to use video analysis.

Video analysis has become much more accessible in recent years, I remember having to advance the frame on a VHS tape player and measure distance with a ruler on the curved screen of a CRT TV when I was an A Level student! It is often a more versatile tool than light gates, however, like all techniques it does have its own limitations.

Before you start this practical, install *tracker* open source physics software on your computer. If you do not have access to a PC or mac find a video analysis app on your phone or tablet, I use *vidanalysis free* on my phone and it's good enough for quick tracking of motion.

There is a full guide to installing and using *tracker* here: http://physlets.org/tracker/help/frameset.html (note: it's a very powerful tool used for University level study, so you don't need to learn everything it can do! You can if you are interested, but it's more than we need at A Level Physics.)

I have two videos explaining how to use these pieces of software, you can find them by searching *gorillaphysics video analysis* or by following the two links below:

Tracker on Computer: https://youtu.be/HeDSjmWw_Fs *Video Analysis - "Tracker"*

Smart Phone or Tablet: https://youtu.be/Vgcf0G61nLg *Phone Physics Video Analysis*

Method

1. Decide on a motion that you want to track, it could be as simple as a falling ball, or a ball rolling down a hill. Ideally it would be something where you would expect a constant acceleration. But it might be more interesting to analyse a sport or the motion of a remote-controlled car. *Have you ever wondered how fast you can throw a ball, or the speed of your tennis serve?* Now you have the tools to find out!

2. Video your chosen situation, remember to keep the camera as still as possible. It is best to prop it up or use a tripod if available. If possible, have a contrasting background, so the position of your object will be sharp against it.

3. Follow the video tutorial or the instructions on the tracker help website above to track the motion of your object. Essentially the steps to video analysis go; *import video, calibrate length, create point mass, click its position every frame of your video, analyse graphs or export data to a spreadsheet for analysis.*

Analysis

1. Use tracker to generate a displacement vs time graph, a velocity vs time graph and an acceleration vs time graph.
2. Think about the speeds and accelerations that your graphs show and comment whether they seem sensible compared to other everyday speeds. Hint; think about roughly how many metres you cover in a second whilst walking or riding a bike.
3. Use your velocity vs time graph to discuss the acceleration of your object. *What value was it? Was it constant?* If your velocity vs time graph curves use tangents at various points to calculate the changes in acceleration throughout the motion. Use your knowledge about forces to explain the changes in acceleration throughout the motion. Hint: you may want to print the graphs out to be able to do some of this analysis by hand, or otherwise export the data to excel, as tracker does not give you an option to create a line of best fit.

Questions

1. How are the three motion graphs related to each other? Think about the gradients and the areas of each graph.
2. Why do you think it is that the graphs get less precise each time you divide position by time? Hint: this is called compounding an uncertainty and it's a key principle in practical physics.
3. State what is meant by an object showing uniform acceleration. Find the four equations of uniform acceleration by research and define the terms.
4. Sketch a displacement time graph velocity time graph and acceleration time graph for a ball bouncing. If you would like to do this more precisely you could take measurements from this photo. The flags on the clamp stand are 20cm apart and the stroboscopic flashes are set at 20Hz.

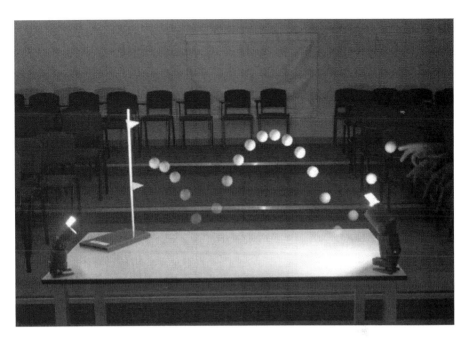

5. A car accelerates from 5m/s to 10m/s to overtake a tractor on a country road, it takes 3 seconds for that acceleration to happen. Calculate the distance covered by the car during the acceleration.

6. A ball bearing is fired straight up at a speed of 40 m/s, calculate the time during which it is in the air. Ignore air resistance.

7. Derive the three equations of Motion from the equation linking speed distance and time and the definition of acceleration.

Answers

1. Here are the three graphs for a constant positive acceleration of 5m/s².

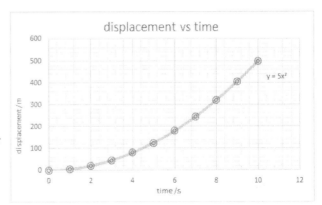

displacement vs time

$y = 5x^2$

displacement / m

time / s

The values displayed on the velocity-time graph are the gradients of the displacement-time graph. The values displayed on the acceleration time graph are the gradients of the velocity-time graph. The area underneath the acceleration time graph is the final velocity. The area underneath velocity time graph distance travelled.

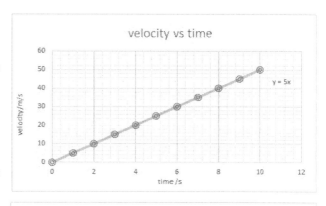

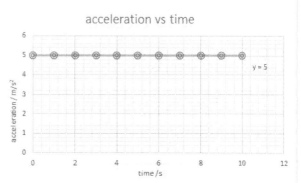

If you are studying maths at A-Level as well it would be useful to relate this to the ideas of differentiation which essentially gives you an equation for a gradient at any point, and integration which gives you an equation to calculate the area underneath a graph. I have left the equations on the graphs so that you can do the calculus and work between them if you are so inclined! (Great pun! Get it? Rise over run = incline…. $\frac{dy}{dx}$ = gradient. Lols, maths.)

Why not challenge yourself to sketch the graphs for a constant negative acceleration, or even a changing acceleration.

2. There is an uncertainty in both the position recorded each time you click the mouse and an uncertainty in the time between each frame. It is likely that the uncertainty in the position is larger than the uncertainty in time, as it is sometimes difficult to click exactly the same point on the object especially if it is blurred in the frame. Each time the program makes a subsequent calculation using the measurement

again and so the uncertainty is compounded, i.e it gets larger and larger. When we compound uncertainties, we add the percentage uncertainties, this is something that students quite find quite tricky at a level at first but with practice it becomes second nature.

3. Uniform acceleration is motion where the acceleration is constant, i.e. it doesn't change for a given period of time. It is also called linear motion. The equations of uniform acceleration can only be used for situations where the acceleration is constant. Most real-world situations do not have a constant acceleration so you'll often be told to ignore resistive forces that like air resistance and friction which change as velocity changes. In many cases, even though it is an approximation it is still a useful model.

$$v = u + at$$

$$s = \frac{1}{2}(u + v)t$$

$$s = ut + \frac{1}{2}at^2$$

$$v^2 = u^2 + 2as$$

s = displacement (sometimes given symbols x, y, or z if motion)

u = initial velocity

v = final velocity

a = acceleration

t = time

These are often called the suvat equations because of the algebraic symbols used.

Pro-tip: Just like at GCSE mechanics topics can seem impossibly hard at first. There's just so much new maths to get your head around.

Focus on learning the fundamental skills of answering any numerical question: Identify the data that you have been given, the data you've been asked to calculate, select an equation, rearrange, convert units and input them, calculate and check.

Then just keep practicing and eventually mechanics will be one of your strongest areas!

4. The graphs for a ball bouncing under gravity are counter intuitive at first. To really follow them you just need to understand that the ball is at a constant acceleration except during the bounce, i.e. when it is accelerated upwards by the surface it is bouncing on.

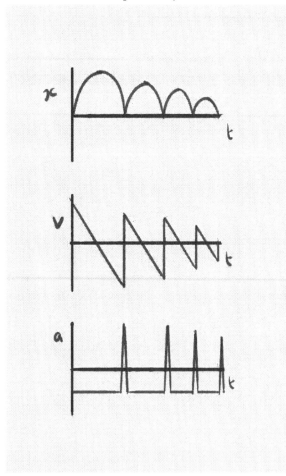

This is often called a saw tooth graph and it surprises students at first and is often used to test the deeper understanding of how gradients are related to one another in the three motion graphs. Focus on understanding the idea that the acceleration of the situation is gravitational acceleration and so it is always -9.81m/s² and so the gradient of the velocity time graph is a constant and negative, with very small periods of time showing large positive accelerations during the bounces.

5. $s = \frac{1}{2}(u + v)t$

$s = \frac{1}{2} \times (5 + 10) \times 3$

$s = 22.5m$

6. $v = u + at$

$v - u = at$

$$\frac{v - u}{a} = t$$

$$\frac{0 - 40}{-9.81} = t$$

$t = 4.08s$

$time\ of\ flight = 8.15s$

4.08s is the time to the top of the flight, so total time of flight is 8.15s. This thinking is the root to solving all projectiles questions, the key information in the question is the information you are not told, but which you know. In this case, a = g = - 9.81m/s² and final velocity, i.e. the velocity at the top of the flight is zero. These bits of *hidden* data are often used to add extra challenge into questions.

7. velocity $v = \frac{s}{t}$ acceleration $a = \frac{v-u}{t}$

i. Rearrange $a = \frac{v-u}{t}$ to give $v = u + at$

ii. Rearrange $v = \frac{s}{t}$ to give $s = vt$ total distance for an accelerating object would be average speed multiplied by time so $s = \frac{1}{2}(u + v)t$

iii. Substitute $v = u + at$ into $s = \frac{1}{2}(u + v)t$ and expand the bracket to give $s = ut + \frac{1}{2}at^2$

iv. Rearrange $a = \frac{v-u}{t}$ to give $t = \frac{v-u}{a}$, substitute into $s = \frac{1}{2}(u + v)t$ expand and simplify to give $v^2 = u^2 + 2as$

Pro-tip: Deriving is a skill that you get better at with practice. Find as many derivations as you can in your textbook and practice them until you can do them without looking. Make sure you learn any derivations by heart that are identified in your specification.

---

2. Time Period of a Pendulum

Data logging used to be the preserve of the adventurous, forward thinking Physics teacher, seen by others as practicing some dark art! Classes would gather round a jumble of wires, boxes, and the one school computer which had the software installed on it, to watch the teacher try and recall which wire goes where, or which settings they were supposed to use for this experiment. When, and if, the thing actually got going they would watch as it plotted a graph, or gave some very high precision value for time and then return to their seats not really knowing what they'd seen but ready to write, *well... you could use data logging* as an answer to an evaluative question in an exam.

Now that every student in a class has a powerful smartphone in their pockets, much of the aging data logging equipment that schools have is redundant. Used well, smartphone data logging can give you very quick, accurate, quantified conclusions or even data which you can export to do in depth analysis on.

From the app store download an app called *physics toolbox*. This basically gives you access to the sensors in your smartphone. There are loads of different functions and sets of data that you can get out of this app, but we are going to use one called a linear accelerometer. I introduce the app in a video called *phone physics data logging* which you can search for or find here: https://youtu.be/NBPWPULoudI

You are going to make a simple pendulum out of string and some form of holder for your phone. You will vary the length of the Pendulum and see how the time period varies. Make a sling to hold your phone in, this could be as simple as a piece of card would you fold and tape together and attach to the end of the pendulum string. Make sure that your phone is either in a case or that you're doing this over a carpeted area so you don't damage the phone should it drop out.

Open the app and set it on to linear accelerometer. Move it around a little; flat, vertically and side to side and notice the coloured x, y and z graphs. These are the three dimensions of space and a lot of Physics will involve analysing vectors in these dimensions. This time though, as your phone will likely twist as it swings, you can just use the white graph, which is the modulus of the acceleration, a scalar version of the 3 accelerations.

Method

1. Decide on a range of lengths of Pendulum perhaps something between 1 m and 10 cm.
2. Hang pendulum apparatus from the longest length, start the linear accelerometer app and let your pendulum swing freely from a small angle.
3. Use the graph on the physics toolbox app to calculate a time period, which is the time taken for one full swing of the pendulum. You can pause the recording you can zoom in to one full cycle of the graph, or you could use the graph to find the time for ten full swings and divide this by ten to give you one time period. You could even export the data and analyse it in something like Google sheets or Excel.
4. Repeat the experiment for different lengths of the Pendulum within your range, try to get at least 7 good data points.

Analysis

1. What shape of graph do you get from the smartphone?
2. Plot a graph of length, l, versus time period, T. Think about the shape of this graph and think if there are any equations for graphs that are similar in shape to this one.
3. Now plot time period squared against length, T^2 vs l, and comment on the shape of this graph. What does this show about the relationship between the two variables?
4. Comment on the spread of data from your line of best fit on your graph. Think if there are any ways you could improve this precision. Perhaps even conduct the experiment again using this stopwatch to

measure 10 full swings and dividing that time by 10 to give you the time period.

5. Think about where you measured your length from and to. What does this say about the validity of your results?

6. Repeat the experiment once more and allow your pendulum amplitude to decrease to near zero. Use ideas about conservation of energy to explain this decrease in amplitude. Think of ways that you could speed up this decline in amplitude or allow the Pendulum to swing for longer.

7. Now go play in the park on a set of swings, and use one of the two methods of accurate timing we've come across to measure the time period of a swing!

Questions

1. Apart from length what other variable do you think affects the time period of a pendulum? Hint: you may like to research the equation for time period of a pendulum.

2. Design a practical to test your hypothesis from question 1.

3. The pendulum in a grandfather clock takes two seconds to complete a full cycle, calculate the length of the Pendulum.

4. The grandfather clock from question 3 is moved to the moon. Calculate how long it takes for the second-hand to go around the clock once. The gravitational field strength on the moon is 1.6N/kg.

5. Sketch a graph of displacement vs time, then velocity vs time, then acceleration vs time for a simple pendulum through 3 full swings. Comment on the shape of these graphs.

6. Look back at your notes for analysis point 6. You should have seen the graph continue sinusoidally with a decreasing amplitude. How does the time period change over this decline in amplitude? This decline in amplitude is called damping; by research define damping and suggest two examples of when it would be beneficial to damp periodic motion.

7. Pendulums are an example of periodic Simple Harmonic Motion (SHM). Use research to define SHM and use you graphs from

question 5 to explain how you know that your pendulum was undergoing SHM.

Answers

1. Only the length affects the time period of a pendulum here on earth, the other variable is gravitational acceleration. The time period is proportional to the root of the left the root of 1 over gravitational acceleration. We call this the pendulum equation.

$$T = 2\pi \sqrt{\frac{l}{g}}$$

   However it is easy to think that the mass would affect the time period of a pendulum, you can accidentally arrive at evidence for mass being a factor because many ways of adding mass change the centre of mass of the pendulum bob and so effectively change the length of the pendulum. Therefore, it's important to note that you measure the length between the pivot and the centre of mass of the pendulum bob. Also, you could be forgiven for thinking that the amplitude of a pendulum affects the time period, but as pendulum motion is simple harmonic the amplitude does not affect the time period. However we do say that a pendulum's motion is simple harmonic for small amplitudes because if you raise the initial position of the pendulum bob above the pivot and release it you will get some effects where the string slackens and then tenses, it does a sort of whipping motion which changes the behaviour of Pendulum.

2. These can be some of the hardest questions, you have to design your own practical. They would usually be worth about 6 Marks and potentially you'd have two marks by identifying independent variable dependent variable and control variables. Two marks for taking your variables and suggesting how to use them to plot a straight-line graph in form $y = mx + c$. Potentially two marks for your description of accurate technique of repetition, identifying anomalies and averaging

results, to avoid random uncertainty and maybe an assessment of the risk and safety precaution if relevant.

Your answer to question 2 will be based on your hypothesis from question 1; if you thought the mass would affect the pendulum then that should be your independent variable, or if you thought the release angle would affect the time period then that should be your independent variable.

You should state explicitly your dependent variable and how you are going to measure it. This is likely to be the time period of the Pendulum either using 10 swings and dividing by 10 or by using some sort of motion tracking technology to allow greater precision.

You should state that you are planning on plotting independent variable against the time period and seeing if there is a relationship. You could use inspection of the trend that results to establish proportionality, hence establish a constant and hence prove a rule. However if you correctly determined that only gravitational acceleration and length affect the time period, Then you would need to design experiment where that you visited other planets or moons, or conduct the practical in the microgravity of a satellite of Earth. It is not beyond the realms of possibility to design a small probe with a pendulum in it to visit other celestial bodies or which changes its position relative to Earth to change its gravitational field strength.

3. By research find the equation $T = 2\pi\sqrt{\frac{l}{g}}$

$$T^2 = 4\pi^2 \frac{l}{g}$$

$$\frac{T^2 g}{4\pi^2} = l$$

$$\frac{2^2 \times 9.81}{4\pi^2} = l$$

$$l = 0.994m$$

4. By research find g on the moon to be 1.63m/s².

   Calculate time period from equation:

   $$T = 2\pi\sqrt{\frac{l}{g}}$$

   $$T = 2\pi\sqrt{\frac{0.994}{1.63}}$$

   $$T = 4.91s$$

   Each full swing moves second hand on twice, so 30 full swings take the second hand around once. $30 \times 4.91 = 147s$

5. Displacement vs time is a cosine graph, (if starting from maximum displacement.)

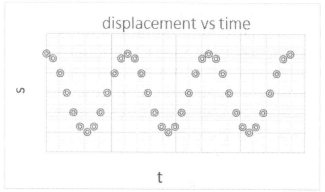

Velocity vs time graph is a negative sine graph, i.e. it's the gradient of the displacement vs time graph.

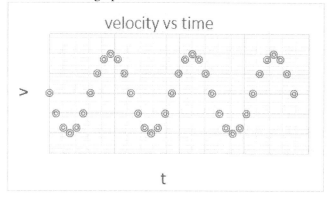

Acceleration vs time graph is a negative cosine graph, i.e. it's the gradient of the velocity vs time graph.

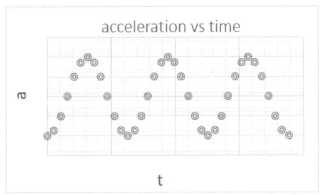

Think about how we discovered motion graphs were related in experiment 1. When you draw this type of graph it is a good idea to draw them directly above one another and use your ruler to line up the key points. The most important things are to line up the stationary points with the points of maximum gradient below. And pay close attention to whether the points and gradients are positive or negative. Mark on the key points then draw your line through those points!

6. The time period for a simple pendulum is not affected by the amplitude. Damping involves adding a device to a structure to absorb energy during each swing. In reality all simple harmonic motion is damped to a degree as we cannot produce an entirely friction free machine, and so some energy is transferred to heat in the surroundings in every oscillation. There are many examples of motions to which damping systems are added. The millennium bridge in London is one example, when it was brand new the bridge oscillated with very high amplitudes as pedestrians naturally fell in step as they walked across, damping systems were added and now it shows only very slight motion. Cars' interiors need to be designed with damping systems in place, otherwise car journeys would be a terrible annoyance, with very loud vibrations occurring at many speeds and engine frequencies.

7. The definition of Simple Harmonic Motion (SHM) is that *there is an acceleration always towards an equilibrium position and proportional to the displacement from the equilibrium position.* The oscillation must also have a constant time period which is independent of the acceleration. For example, our bouncing ball from the questions in experiment one is not SHM. Fascinatingly, all this definition can be summed up with the equation $F = -k\Delta x$. The force in the equation is proportional to acceleration so can be seen as the acceleration for a given mass, the minus sign is very important in this case as it signifies *towards* and the k just signifies some constant due to the system.

We know this motion is SHM as there is a constant time period, and the displacement vs time graph is a cosine graph, whilst the acceleration time graph is a minus cosine graph (reflected in the time axis.) This shows acceleration towards the equilibrium position and proportional to the displacement from the equilibrium position.

Pro-tip: SHM graphs are a complicated application of something very simple, relating equations to graphs.

Practice this skill, it runs through all of A Level Physics, and when you get good at it you can communicate many ideas, hypotheses and conclusions by making sketch graphs!

Some notable examples where equations are linked to graphs are listed below:

The rules regarding gradients and areas in motion graphs; s vs t — gradient is the velocity, v vs t gradient is the acceleration, area under is the distance travelled.

The gradients of V-I characteristic graphs in electricity represent the inverse of the resistance.

Force-extension graphs have gradients equal to the spring constant and stress vs strain graphs have gradients equal to the Young modulus in material properties.

All exponential graphs; see experiment 3!

---

3. Half-Life of a Two Litre Bottle of Water

You will most likely have modelled the random nature of radioactive decay in the classroom by using large numbers of dice. You may even have measured the half-life of protactinium. In physics you will find that many relationships follow a very similar trend to the decay of radioactive nuclei. Think of the standard half-life graph that you be used to from GCSE physics. We call that type of decline exponential decay, and radioactive decay is only one example from A level Physics.

The simplest way to describe exponential decay is that for any given length of time the ratio of the value of starting y variable to final y variable is the same. We say exponentials are *equal ratios in equal times.* That is why we use the term *half-life* meaning the time taken for any y variable to half is a constant. In A Level Physics you will need to take the analysis further and deal with any given net decline. Use this experiment as your first analysis of an exponential function.

In this experiment you will use water pressure to model exponential decay, and importantly you will use spreadsheets to analyse your results, which is an invaluable skill in A Level Physics.

Read the method carefully and think if there are ways you can make your readings more accurate before you start. You could do a trial run to decide how to measure time and how to use repeated readings to reduce the effect of random uncertainty. Decide a good interval for the time, you want something close enough together to give you at least ten data points, but not so close together that you cannot measure the time and distance accurately.

One of the main sources of uncertainty will be in measuring the height of water, so consider how to accurately use your ruler to avoid parallax error. I've gone through this experiment in this video you can watch here, it might give some ideas to make your experiment as successful as possible.

Half life of a bottle of water https://youtu.be/b7jmWk4cdXA

Method

1. Take an empty 2L bottle, carefully use something sharp to bore a hole in the very bottom of it.
2. Cover the hole up with Blu-Tack or tape or just keep your finger over the hole whilst you fill the bottle with water.
3. Allow the bottle to empty over the sink and measure height of water above the hole continuously at intervals of 15s, recording these into a spreadsheet.

Analysis

1. Use Excel's *insert chart* function to plot an *x-y scatter* chart of your results.
2. Select the data and ask Excel to plot a line of best fit, this is called a *trendline* in Excel. Notice it defaults to a straight line, but you can use the options panel to change it to exponential line. This is what we expect to fit the data but if you find one of the other curves fit the data better then you should use that. If you find it impossible to fit a curve, then you should print the sheet and draw the curve as normal by hand.
3. Now use the graph to calculate a half-life. As half-life is defined as the average time taken by the height to decline by half, use the graph to calculate half-life using multiple points on a graph.
4. We would always where possible like to resolve our theory so that we achieve a straight-line graph. This is because using a gradient as a type of graphical average takes less account of anomalies than an arithmetic mean does. In this case if you take the natural log of the height variable, and plot that against time you should get a straight-line graph, with a negative gradient. Use Excel to make a second table *ln(h)* versus *t*, and plot a graph of that.
5. Use ideas about pressure to discuss why the rate of flow of water decreases over time.
6. Consider how accurate the model is as a representation of exponential decay.

Questions

1. Protactinium has a half-life of 71 seconds, calculate the time it would take for a sample to decrease from 48Bq to 3Bq.

2. According to the mathematical model of radioactive decay, any given sample of a radioactive isotope would never become inactive explain why this is true in theory but is not true in practice.

3. Use this student's data to plot a decay curve, use the graph to estimate a half-life.

t /s	counts per 15 s			Average per 15s
0	69	56	51	
15	56	39	64	
30	48	40	52	
45	48	41	52	
60	37	35	35	
75	36	20	33	
90	30	25	28	
105	29	24	22	
120	16	23	28	
135	22	20	18	
150	21	26	20	
165	18	19	24	
180	19	10	23	

4. Comment on whether there are any anomalies.

5. Resolve the data into a straight-line graph. Use the same technique as we used in the analysis of the water bottle decay data.

6. Calculate the gradient of the line. The magnitude of this gradient is known as the time constant or decay constant, and we use the symbol λ (lambda) to represent it.

7. Use the equation $A = A_0 e^{-\lambda t}$ to calculate activity in counts per 15s at time 100s. A is the activity that you are trying to calculate and A_0 is the activity at time zero (i.e. the y intercept of your exponential graph.)

8. Use the relationship $t_{1/2} = \frac{ln2}{\lambda}$ to calculate a half-life. Compare the value estimated from the graph in question 3 with this value. Which do you think is more accurate and why? Hint: compare as a percentage difference between the calculated values and the accepted value of half-life for protactinium (question 1). Suggest any possible reasons for inaccuracy in your calculation of half-life.

Answers

1. 4 half lives have passed. $4 \times 71 = 284s$ The shortcut to doing this type of sum is to make $\frac{3}{48} = 0.5^x$, where x is the number of half lives we want to calculate, then take log to base ½ of both sides giving

$$log_{\frac{1}{2}} \frac{3}{48} = x = 4$$

2. An exponential decay graph has a set time for a set net decline, e.g. the time taken for a value to half is constant and is called the half-life. Therefore whatever the original value of activity the final value would approach zero, but never get there. In reality there are only a set number of radioactive nuclei, each has a certain probability of decaying each second, so eventually all the nuclei will have decayed. You could also talk about it only being possible to have whole numbers of radioactive nuclei.

3.

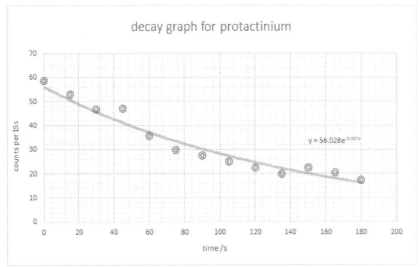

decay graph for protactinium

$y = 56.028e^{-0.007x}$

counts per 15s

time /s

Notice that the coefficient of the exponential number is the y intercept.

Use interpolation at 28 gives approximately 100s.

4. Anomalies must be very far from mean, and defining an anomaly depends on the general scatter around the mean. In this case the data is all very scattered, so it would not be appropriate to treat any of the data as an anomaly. In other words, if repeats tend to fall very precisely around a mean then anomaly needs only be slightly away from the mean, whereas if the data is not very precise it takes a very large distance from the mean to qualify as an anomaly. Also 3 repeats is not a very large data set, so this makes it more difficult to spot an anomaly and therefore a lower precision of data will need to be tolerated.

Pro-tip: Exponential decays come up in many areas of A Level Physics. Once you can work with one of them you can do them all!
Equations for exponential decay can be generalised in the form:
$$y = y_0 e^{-\mu x}$$ *where μ is the general form of the decay constant*
Taking logs gives: $\ln y = \ln y_0 - \mu x$ which is a graph of a straight line in the
form $y = c - mx$, a straight line with gradient equal to the decay constant.

5.

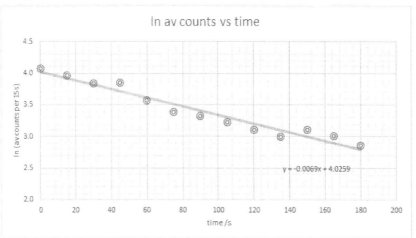

In av counts vs time

$y = -0.0069x + 4.0259$

Notice now that the same value as was the multiplier of the exponent in the exponential curve is now the modulus of the gradient of the graph. The y intercept of our straight line graph is $\ln(A_0)$.

6. This gradient is what we call the decay constant (λ) and is equivalent to the probability of an individual nucleus of protactinium decaying during any given second.

7. $A = A_0 e^{-\lambda t}$

$A = 56 e^{-0.0069 \times 100}$

$A = 28$

8. $t_{1/2} = \dfrac{\ln 2}{\lambda}$

$t_{1/2} = \dfrac{\ln 2}{0.0069}$

$t_{1/2} = 100s$

In my case both of my methods of determining half-life give 100s. This is because I have entirely used excel, a hand drawn graph of decay with this data may yield a different value for half-life. One could potentially remove the point at 45s and the points after 135s as well, although this would be unjustified on the evidence that we have were the true value of half-life not known!

The percentage difference in each of my values for half-life is given by

$\%D = \frac{100-71}{71} = 41\%$, this is very high. Many more repeats would lead

to a similarly too high value for the half-life of protactinium, this is an example of a systematic error. This is most likely due to background radiation.

If we were to repeat this experiment again we might accurately measure average background radiation over 5-10 minutes and deduct that from each of our readings. This is called a corrected count rate. Another way we could get greater accuracy would be to have a much larger sample of our radioisotope, this would mean our error due to background, and our uncertainty due to the random nature of radioactive decay would be reduced as a percentage of our readings. However increasing the activity of the source would make the risks involved greater and the benefit not greatly increased!

Pro-tip: During practical experimentation in the lab there are always lots of little problems that you have to solve, (I find that a handy piece of bluetack is invaluable for holding things in place.) However you do not need to worry about these incidental problems when you describe experiments in an exam.

Stick to simple statements of what you are measuring, what meter you are going to use and what the accurate technique is. You do not need to go into details on how exactly this will be clamped to that, or exactly what practical difficulties you had when you conducted this practical because the apparatus had funny dimensions, or wouldn't fit in place, or you found it was ok to balance this on that etc.

My best advice is to read the exam board method sheets and to use the descriptive terminology that they use. Keep methods concise, refer to detailed diagrams if there is an opportunity to do so, and make sure you've included exactly what they've asked for in the question.

Independent Study Tasks

Independent Study is the Key to Success at A Level!

These 18 tasks, and the few extras which follow, are designed to be completed along side your normal study during the two years at A Level. Don't expect to do them all once, try and pace yourself through them and do about three every term. This way they should follow your study and grow in content and difficulty as your knowledge and skills develop during the course.

Some of the tasks are about keeping you engaged and pointing you at the most interesting parts of the A Level, for example task 10 will help you make a timeline of developments in Astrophysics. Some tasks are designed to keep you experimenting and thinking about the practical principles in Physics that you need for your practical qualification and the exams, for example task 3 will help you measure viscosities at home, (and get pretty messy in doing so!) Some tasks are about building your list of revision materials, for example task 18 will show you how to make notes on each of the experiments, and many of the extra tasks will focus you on revision. Some of the tasks will engage you in exam materials and reviewing your own performance on practice papers, for example task 7 will lead you through analysing your performance on a set of As papers as you approach the end of your first year at A Level.

All of the tasks have been designed by me using my experience of what works to get students the grades. Give them a go, set aside enough time to do a good job of them, and most of all enjoy studying Physics!

Pro-tip: Ask anyone who has studied A Levels; the step up from GCSE to a level is huge. In no subject is this more so than physics. The sheer breadth of knowledge and understanding that A-level students deal with in the two-year course is daunting, but also there is a huge shift in cognitive demand in the assessments. Prepare yourself to work incredibly hard over the next two years and be ready to have to put in the hours to meet the challenge.

---

1 Use the PhET *projectile motion* simulation to come up with a list of factors which effect the range of a projectile.
https://phet.colorado.edu/en/simulation/projectile-motion
Then design a practical that you could conduct to investigate the effect of changing one of them.

PhET SIMS

PhET Sims are some of the best simulations for physics that you can find online, it's a great resource whenever you find it difficult to visualise what is going on in a practical or theory. You can use them all for free at the PhET website, and any that are written into HTML5 you can now have on your phone on an app. This one is just a basic Newtonian physics idea, but they do have them for quantum, nuclear physics and space; and they have loads that go far beyond A level physics.

Experiment

Once you've got the projectile motion app loaded, start with the basic intro and play about with the functions. I suggest you leave air resistance off for all of your experiments with this simulation, as we always model every distance as negligible in A level physics.

Once you think you got an understanding of what everything does then try these simple experiments:

- Set the angle at zero and varying the height at even increments. *Does The range vary evenly as well?*
- Leave the launch height of zero and varying the angle. Answer these questions by experimenting. *Does the range increase linearly with the angle? Is there an angle at which ranges a maximum?*

- Vary the initial speed of your project and keep angle and launch height constant. Again, *does the range very linearly with speed?*

Use the measuring tape to measure range and analyse how the factor you have chosen affects the range of your projectile. Use a spreadsheet to plot graphs. A little bit of research will help you to understand the theory behind the range of projectiles that you can apply to your analysis of the results.

Take it Further

On the *lab* tab of the simulation notice that changing the mass and the diameter the cannonball does not change the range as long as air resistance is off! Galileo?!? ☺ On this page doing something like changing the acceleration due to gravity or making some prediction calculations and then testing them out would be really good way to test out how well you understand this.

This type of thing is not that difficult to code. Using graphing software like *desmos* or a spreadsheet, you can write simulations like this where you can input some values for quantities and the computer will calculate a range or plot a graph to represent the parabola. It just takes a good understanding and ability to apply the equations that you are taught. This will be useful skill to have as you move forward to further education or into your own projects in the future. Give it a try and if you enjoy it you can apply these skills to all the areas of physics that you will learn about.

Anything where you are applying your knowledge and having to solve problems with it, is the best activity for the deepest, most effective learning, and that's what's going to get you the top grades.

Simulations in Real Physics

By far the best use of simulations however is to use them as research for real experiments. Take your time think about what apparatus you have at school and plan out an experiment that you can verify your findings with. Some schools do have projectile launching machines for these experiments, which are just spring-loaded launchers, but I'm sure you could devise something that can fire projectiles at a roughly constant speed. The other common way to launch something at a pretty constant speed is to use curtain rails or ramps as ski jumps for ball bearings or marbles.

Measuring range accurately is a bit more difficult, but I suggest you just keep it simple, fix a metre ruler to ground or table, watch closely where the projectile lands, and mark immediately with a dry wipe marker. Repeated measurements do tend to come out with quite high precision in this simple experiment.

If you have access to light gates at your school, then you can very easily measure launch speed and include that in your calculations. It will be interesting to note how close calculated ranges are to real world measured ones!

Once you have written yourself plan then take it to the teacher, show them discuss your risk assessment with them and ask if you can conduct it! Have fun! It's so easy in year twelve and thirteen to spend all your time worrying about the exams at the end of the course, but remember you aren't studying exams; you're studying physics! Physics *is* the experiments, that's the science and that's where all the enjoyment comes from. Go through your course enjoying yourself and you'll be much more likely to be willing to put the effort in when it comes to revising for those exams.

2 Read and summarise Richard Feynman's lecture on the law of conservation of energy:

http://www.feynmanlectures.caltech.edu/I_04.html

"It is important to realize that in physics today, we have no knowledge of what energy is. We do not have a picture that energy comes in little blobs of a definite amount. It is not that way. However, there are formulas for calculating some numerical quantity, and when we add it all together it gives "28"—always the same number. It is an abstract thing in that it does not tell us the mechanism or the reasons for the various formulas."

Feynman the Great Explainer

List the examples and analogies that Richard Feynman gives in this lecture. Write down any ideas about energy that Richard Feynman gives which surprise you, i.e. they differ from your original understanding of energy.

Then do a little more research on the internet and in your textbook, *do we currently have any better understanding of what energy is?* Evaluate Feynman's lecture on energy and don't be afraid to criticise; ask yourself; does everyone agree with Feynman on energy, is it outdated, has he cut corners, or left out important details that you would prefer to see explained.

Richard Feynman is known as the *great explainer*. You can read all his lectures for free at: http://www.feynmanlectures.caltech.edu/ I strongly suggest that you have a look around, especially when you are struggling to understand a difficult concept in A Level Physics.

You can watch a series he made with the BBC in the 80s called *Fun to Imagine*, in the BBC archive here: https://www.bbc.co.uk/archive/richard-feynman/z6bhd6f (Yes that's what TV was like when I was a kid!) It's a good series though, and it really encapsulates the excitement that you get when you really understand something, in a deep and meaningful way.

3 Measure the viscosity of some household products by conducting a line spread test and/or by measuring the terminal velocity of a rising bubble.

Line Spread Test

Viscosity is a measure of a fluid's resistance to flow; it can be measured either by measuring its rate of flow or by measuring the rate at which something else moves through it. The line spread test is a method of measuring viscosity by measuring the rate of flow of the fluid itself.

Have a look through your cupboards at home for any particularly thick looking fluids, (ask whoever pays for the shopping which stuff they don't mind you wasting them!) I suggest stuff like honey, or treacle, or bottled sauces are good, (if your cupboards are anything like mine there're probably some half-used bottles of condiments that no one really wants to put on their chips lurking around somewhere!) I suggest you don't go with cleaning products like bleach, or anything difficult to clean up as that will lead to safety concerns or worse, an annoyed adult....

You will need:

- a tray to work on, (to keep the mess off the surfaces)
- a small cylindrical container preferably open at both ends, (cut the top off a plastic bottle if you can't find something readymade)
- some paper with a set of axes marked at half centimetre intervals
- some polyethene document wallets
- a stopwatch

Put your paper into the wallet, this is to allow you to wipe the surface after each test, or so that you can just discard and replace the wallets, but it also stops the fluids just being absorbed into the paper.

Fill your cylinder to a set level, holding it down on the origin of the axes so that none spills out from the open bottom end of the cylinder. It doesn't matter how much you use so long as you can use the same volume of each of the fluids that you are going to test.

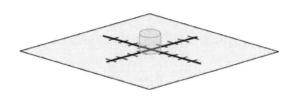

You can decide how long you think it is sensible to time your line spread test for, again, it is not important so long as you do the same for each of the fluids you are going to test. I would suggest about a minute is plenty of time.

Lift the cylinder and start the stopwatch. Take readings of how far the leading edge of the fluid has gone in each of the four directions and calculate an average of these. Repeat this for as many different fluids as you have access to.

Analysis and Evaluation

There isn't much analysis that you can do for this practical except to make some comparisons between your fluids. The least viscous will have travelled the furthest in a given time. You could think about making measurements at different times and being able to graph the rate of flow of your fluid, but this might be overkill for quite a coarse method of determining the viscosity of fluids.

Think about your method and how you could refine it. *Were the volumes that you used large enough to get a good range of readings for your dependant variable? Did you time it for long enough to see the difference between one fluid or the other? Are there any other refinements to this type of method that could make your results more valid?*

A limitation of this method is that you will not be able to find an absolute viscosity. From your results you will be able to rank fluids you test in order from most viscous to least viscous, but you will not be able to find an exact value for the viscosity of any of them. The next method for you to try will allow you to do that.

Terminal Velocity of a Rising Bubble

The falling ball viscometer is a generally specified as a practical for the CPAC part of an A Level course. It uses either manual timing over several successive distances or video analysis to confirm that a ball is falling at terminal velocity. By analysis of the forces in equilibrium we can calculate an absolute viscosity of the fluid that it is falling through. The diagram shows the forces acting on a ball falling through a fluid.

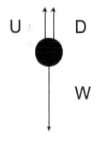

The falling ball viscometer is a method to measure the viscosity of a fluid by measuring the terminal velocity of something moving through it, this is possible because the viscosity will affect the fluid's ability to flow around the object. In this experiment we will use a rising bubble to measure viscosity.

The analysis of the forces at terminal velocity is a difficult derivation which you will come across early in your study of A Level Physics. It seems really complicated but in fact is really simple. I'll take you through it step by step:

Force Analysis for a Falling Ball

write an expression for the forces on a ball falling at terminal velocity (weight, upthrust and drag)	$W = U + D$	(1)
write an expression for the weight of the ball bearing in terms of its density, ρ_b, its radius, r, and gravitational field strength, g	$W = m_b g = \rho_b V g = \frac{4}{3}\pi r^3 \rho_b g$	(2)
write an expression for the upthrust acting on the ball bearing in terms of the density of the fluid, ρ_f, its radius, r, and gravitational field strength, g	$U = m_f g = \rho_f V g = \frac{4}{3}\pi r^3 \rho_f g$	(3)
write an expression for the drag force using Stokes' Law, where η is the coefficient of viscosity and v is the terminal velocity of the ball bearing in the fluid	$D = 6\pi\eta r v$	(4)
insert equations 2, 3 and 4 into equation 1	$\frac{4}{3}\pi r^3 \rho_b g = \frac{4}{3}\pi r^3 \rho_f g + 6\pi\eta r v$	(5)
rearrange	$\frac{4}{3}\pi r^3 \rho_b g - \frac{4}{3}\pi r^3 \rho_f g = 6\pi\eta r v$	(6)

factorise $$\frac{4}{3}\pi r^3 g(\rho_b - \rho_f) = 6\pi\eta r v \tag{7}$$

cancel common factors and simplify fraction $$\frac{2}{9}r^2 g(\rho_b - \rho_f) = \eta v \tag{8}$$

rearrange for viscosity $$\frac{2r^2 g(\rho_b - \rho_f)}{9v} = \eta \tag{9}$$

Force Analysis for a Rising Bubble

In order not to simply repeat the core practical here or otherwise to necessitate slightly more specialised apparatus than most people have at home; namely ball bearings, 0.01g resolution mass balances, magnets and measuring cylinders; we are going to use a rising bubble of air as our object and measure its terminal velocity as it rises through our fluid.

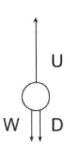

For a bubble rising the drag force is in the same direction as the weight, so much of the derivation is the same but we need to change step 1 and therefore step 6 and step 9 become:

write an expression for the forces on a ball falling at terminal velocity $$W + D = U \tag{1}$$

now ρ_a, the density of air replaces density of the ball for the expression for weight $$\frac{4}{3}\pi r^3 \rho_a g + 6\pi\eta r v = \frac{4}{3}\pi r^3 \rho_f g \tag{5}$$

rearrange $$\frac{4}{3}\pi r^3 \rho_{bf} g - \frac{4}{3}\pi r^3 \rho_a g = 6\pi\eta r v \tag{6}$$

factorise, cancel common factors and simplify fraction, rearrange for viscosity

$$\frac{2r^2 g (\rho_f - \rho_a)}{9v} = \eta \qquad (9)$$

For this method you will need:

- a tall glass or vase
- some translucent fluid which you can pour into the glass
- a ruler and stopwatch, or a camera and computer for video analysis

This works well with washing up liquid, and if you're careful you don't need to waste what you use. You could do this with fizzy drinks which give up their own bubbles, basically anything that you can see a bubble rising in, so long as it doesn't rise so fast that it's impossible to measure accurately. If your bubbles are too fast to measure with a stopwatch then you can adapt this method to use video analysis and you'll be able to get an accurate terminal velocity in that manner. I suggest that you keep it simple though as there is going to be enough data handling even with manual timing.

Mark two lines a measured distance apart on your glass, these are your start and finish lines for your timing. There isn't much of a need to measure over several intervals as the bubbles will be pretty much rising at terminal velocity from the outset, but you can do this if you are not sure. Pour your viscous fluid from as large a height as you can without spilling it, (no need to pour from a height if you are using carbonated beverages,) this allows more air to get in and so creates more bubbles. Closely watch individual bubbles of roughly equal size and time them between your two markers, repeat this a few times for an average.

You'll need to figure out a way to judge the diameter of the bubbles that you measured, using a ruler mounted next to the glass and taking a photo, or using some other type of reference, may be the best way to do this.

You'll also need to find the density of your fluid and of air, make sure these are in kgm^{-3}. The density of air you'll find by research and the fluid you can either use a measuring jug and kitchen scales or find approximate values from the internet. Once you've got all your data you can input it into the formula we derived above.

Analysis and Evaluation

Which bubbles rose more rapidly, the smaller ones or the larger ones? Does that surprise you? It shouldn't in a way because the trend predicted by the formula would be that the larger bubbles would rise fastest, however it is a counter intuitive idea! It should teach you to trust the maths, rather than your intuitions, when making predictions or conclusions.

Consider what introduces the most uncertainty into your results and suggest ways to reduce this. Comment whether your suggestions would be practical at home. By research find out the limitations of this method and explain why this method only works for spherical objects at low speeds.

Have a look into the various methods that they use to measure viscosity of fluids in industry, there are many and it's an important thing to get right in manufacturing processes from making jellybeans to laying the foundations of skyscrapers!

It may surprise you to learn that there are whole careers spent refining the size of bubbles in various carbonated drinks, it makes a difference to the way that the drink feels in the mouth! There is a whole branch of Physics dedicated to perfecting confectionary manufacturing, play your cards right and this could be the career for you! Take your pick, fundamental Physicist at CERN or Physicist in charge of the squishiness of flumps! ☺

4 Pick something from *The Student Room*'s reading list for A Level Physics or pick a book from the Physics section of the school library and read it. Write a simple book review for a friend and then swap books with them.

https://www.thestudentroom.co.uk/revision/physics/recommended-physics-reading

Get Interested

I want to leave this really open for you! Find an area of Physics that you love and choose a piece of wider reading that you are keen to read. I have some suggestions of the topics and some books that are accessible enough for you to enjoy. But I strongly suggest that you do a little research and chose your own, otherwise, if you aren't that interested, you'll almost certainly not bother to finish it!

Some Suggestions

It would be a good idea to read something about quantum or astrophysics because these are tricky conceptually. Getting an introduction to them when there's no pressure is a good idea. Hopefully when you do tackle them in class you have more reasons to be interested in the detail you have to learn for your exams.

Try these if you are not sure:

- *Quantum Theory Cannot Hurt You* - Marcus Chown
- *How to Teach Quantum Physics to Your Dog* – Chad Orzel
- *How to Destroy the Universe: And 34 other really interesting uses of physics* – Paul Parsons
- *Chernobyl: History of a Tragedy* – Serhii Plokhy
- *Why does E=mc²?* - Brian Cox and Jeff Forshaw

Another great place to look would be *Primrose Kitten*'s suggested reading for physics page:

https://www.primrosekitten.com/collections/reading-for-a-level-physics

Share Your Interest

Once you've read your book go ahead and tell someone about it.

Maybe you can't recommend it at all, maybe the language was just too high level for you at this stage in your education, maybe actually felt the explanations were poor and the writing was dry and boring. Whatever you thought, tell someone!

Or maybe you loved it and felt it was perfect and everybody who's got a GCSE in science should read this book! Maybe you just felt that your classmates should all read chapter three because when your teacher explained that part of quantum you all left scratching your head wondering what just happened.

In any case reading and discussing being interested in physics is one of the most important things you can do to make sure that you get the highest possible grades. So do it and enjoy it!

The Student Room

The Student Room forum is an amazing resource but be aware of trolls! The recommended reading thread is well maintained and full of great suggestions from young people for books they have actually read. There are loads more examples like that!

However there are also some pernicious people, who just want to spread a little misinformation. Sometimes you'll read things about how easy some people are finding A Levels, or what amazing score they got on Oxbridge tests, or the worst, quick fixes or ways to cheat; steer clear of this nonsense. If you aren't sure of the advice given look for the advice of people like myself on *GorillaPhysics*, Jen at *Primrose Kitten*, or Lewis at *A Level Physics Online*.

5 Make one of your PAG lab reports into an explainer video. Make sure that it's detailed enough that a student who has not conducted the practical could do it, present your own results and conclusion and make sure it has a detailed evaluation.

The Feynman Technique to Learn Anything

Take it from me it's not easy to make explainer videos! But making videos forces you to think very carefully about what you're going to say and how you're going to put across details in a coherent explanation. It's basically the Feynman technique to learn anything; that is *to explain it out loud*.

The Feynman technique works because when you don't understand what you are explaining you stop, … and pause, you um … and err. It makes you realise what you do and don't understand. It forces you to think more carefully about *how* you are explaining the thing. It forces you to think about the order in which you say things and what you leave out and what you put in. It puts you on the spot and it focuses your mind. This all makes for memorable learning experiences and helps you retain details for longer.

Making the Video

Explain the experiment you conducted in a video form. There are loads of ways you can do this! You don't have to be on camera yourself you don't have to talk if you're worried about your voice, (it's much better for your learning if you do talk it through yourself; at the very least though write a script and have somebody else record a voice over.)

You can use your existing results tables and graphs by taking photos, scans or screen shots of them. You can use photos or short videos of the experimental setup. You can put *PowerPoint* slides on screen or handwrite over the screen using a tablet or smartphone. You can do a little bit of stop motion animation or you can use stock footage and images taken from the internet.

There are loads of different free video editing apps on PC, Mac or on smart phones. I really like *Adobe Premiere Rush*, *Kinemaster*, or if you want to try something pro and free then try *daVinci Resolve*, but if you have them already then *Windows Movie Maker* or *iMovie* are absolutely fine for this type of project. You don't need to get bogged down in learning how software works, unless you are interested in developing this important and useful skill for your future!

What to Include in a Lab Report

Whenever you do a lab report for a PAG, Core or Required Practical in A Level Physics then work through the standard scientific model paragraphs. Here's a list of those key headings and a brief description of what each one should be. I suggest that you write up some of your experiments in this level of detail, but you will not have time to do this for all of them! Task 18 is a task to make notes on each of the experiments in your course so that you can memorise the detail that you need for your exams.

Abstract - A good way just to give an overview of what your independent and dependent variables were; and what your findings were. In academic journals these summarise the experiment and let readers decide whether they need to read on to find the details. (You won't be able to write this until you have finished the rest of the report.)

Aim - This is what you're hoping to find out and should be normally phrased as a question that can be tested. For example; *What is the relationship between force and current for a current carrying wire in a magnetic field?*

Research - Concisely present a review of current understanding of the topic you are investigating. Practice using academic referencing techniques, as you need to demonstrate this for your practical qualification, and it is an important skill for University. For books; give the full title, author, ISBN number, date and location of first publishing. For websites; give the title of the page, the URL, and date accessed. If the experiment is to measure a constant, then you should give the accepted value of that constant, verified and referenced from at least two places. It's also worth looking into real world contexts for this science that you are doing. We don't do science in isolation, the results of scientific experiment must contribute to society in some way, or we don't bother to fund the experiement! Find out why it is worth us accurately measuring this constant or knowing this rule, law or equation that you have set out to find!

Prediction - This is what you expect to happen, the relationship you expect to see.

Hypothesis - This contains the justification of your prediction. In physics that would normally refer to some equations containing the variables that you are testing and those that you are controlling, and a prediction of the shape of graph you might expect given equations that you mentioned.

Diagram - A simple two-dimensional representation of the experimental setup using conventional symbols for apparatus where possible and labelling other parts of the setup where there is no conventional symbol. It is best to include dimensions of things in setup such that somebody wanting to repeat the experiment could set-up apparatus exactly the same as you did.

Method - A brief step-by-step method to allow somebody to conduct the practical exactly the same as you did. Include values of any variables that you are controlling.

Accurate Techniques - This detail can be written in the method but it's sometimes useful have a discrete section for it. Here is where you include the techniques that you're going to use to ensure that your measured values are accurate as possible. I suggest you don't just make them up but use the ones explained to you in textbooks, instructional videos or exam board method sheets because they will be the ones that come up in exams.

Predicted Uncertainties - It's good practice to predict uncertainties before the experiment takes place. You can usually use half a scale division the meter you are measuring with as your absolute uncertainty, but that might not always be appropriate. For example, half a scale division on a stopwatch is 0.005s, whereas reaction time is in the order 0.2s! Whatever the absolute uncertainty you choose, justify it. Calculate predicted percentage uncertainties and combine those percentage uncertainties into a compound uncertainty for your final answer. From there calculate a range of acceptable values for your final calculated result to review in your evaluation.

Risk Assessment - A brief discussion of the hazards and their associated risks involved in conducting this experiment. Do not make up or overstate the risks! It is acceptable to state that there are no significant risks in this experiment if that is the case! If there are significant risks, explain what measures you will take to reduce them.

Results – This should include all your raw data and any processed data calculated given to the same significant figures as the data was measured to. Make sure you have correct headings and units. You can identify your anomalies in the table, but you should still present them.

Analysis - This will be your graph of independent variable versus dependent variable, then another graph of your variables processed such that you get a proportional graph with a meaningful gradient. For example, if you're expecting y to be proportional to x^2 then plot y versus x^2 and if you do indeed get a straight line then you have evidence for that relationship.

Conclusion - A conclusion is a review of the hypothesis given the evidence that you collected in your practical. This is a good point to state your final calculated values.

Evaluation - This should certainly be the longest piece of writing in the report. Luckily, it's the most interesting part of an experiment and it's the bit where you get the most creative. Evaluation is one of the hardest skills that we test in exams, so being fluent in writing evaluations gives you the best chance of getting the highest grades. I suggest you work through each of these keywords and consider each question below. This will structure your writing and ensure that you use those keywords correctly in exams.

Accuracy – Accuracy is defined as the difference between a measured value and a true value. Accuracy is affected by the apparatus and techniques that you choose. Calculate a percentage difference between your final value and the accepted, or true, value. This is your accuracy. One way to think about whether your experiment has been successful or not is to answer the question; *does your percentage difference fall within your predicted percentage uncertainty?* If it does, then you been accurate enough with the apparatus and techniques available. If it didn't, then you should review your methodology and suggest improvements you could make. It's always worth suggesting improvements in any case.

There are two categories of error; random and systematic. Random errors are the only ones that will be improved by repeating measurements, identifying and excluding anomalies, and calculating averages. Systematic error will not be improved by repeating measurement, it will require a change to the system, so a change to the method or apparatus.

Review the trend on your graph at this point, *did you see the curve or the line that you expected?* Often in physics our result is a gradient of a graph. If your results lie on a straight line but gradient is either too steep or too shallow, this can give you clues as to what is going wrong in your experiment. This might be a systematic error which an improvement can remove from the experiment, or which you can account for in your final answer. *Was there a y intercept when there shouldn't have been?* This might help you consider whether there has been any form of zero error. Although if your result is the gradient that may not have affected your final calculated value because it will have just shifted the graph up or down.

Precision - Precision is a measure of the scatter of repeated values around a mean. The more closely grouped your repeats are the more precise your results are. Precision is not the same as resolution, although resolution can have an impact on precision, they do not mean the same thing. Make a comment on how precise your results were and think about how that could be improved. It's also possible to get an idea of precision from a graph, a precise trend will have datapoints lying very close to a line of best fit, whereas an imprecise trend will have points scattered far from the line of best fit. It will be easier to spot a line of best fit the more precise your results are.

This is also the time to review your uncertainties. Once we have results, we can use the range of repeated values for an indication of how certain we are. Take half the range for each value as being your absolute uncertainty. Calculate percentage uncertainties and compound these to give a percentage uncertainty in your final answer. Use this to calculate an absolute uncertainty of that final value and state the value in the form $x = \bar{x} \pm \Delta x$ (where x is the quantity being measured, $\bar{x}$ is your calculated value and Δx is the absolute uncertainty.) Again, it is good practice to compare this to your predicted uncertainties. This might seem like an awful lot of calculations, and it is, but we can use spreadsheets to make this type of thing very quick and easy.

Reliability - Reliability is less used in the newer specifications for exams but, I think it's still a useful concept, It's the idea of how consistent our results or findings are with those of others. But you do have to separate them into two different ideas; repeatability and reproducibility.

Repeatability is the idea that you could do exactly the same experiment and get the same *results*. Answer the question; *if somebody followed my method would they get exactly the same values in their results table as mine?* If not, discuss how this repeatability could be improved. This is likely to be based around the details that you supplied in your method and about how easy it is to control those variables you've identified as other factors affecting the results. Always think about the equations that relate to the practical.

Reproducibility is the idea that somebody else could do a different but related experiment and come to the same conclusion. Ask yourself; *if somebody were to select a different independent variable, select different values for control variables, or follow a different method, would they come to same trend same, or the same final value that you calculated?*

Validity - This is the biggest idea in experimental science; but start with something easy that you will be familiar with, *was the experiment a fair test? Did you control the variables that you set out to? Were some harder to control than you thought?* One way to test this is; if results did not come out as a straight line when the theory suggests that they should, then there is likely to be in another variable influencing those results.

Next reconsider the contexts that you identified in your research and explain what your findings mean in *those contexts*. This is an important thing for scientists to consider, because without any real-world application our science is useless! Without science being useful for society, industry or business then science isn't funded.

Finally ask yourself; *what's next? What further investigations could you do? Did you meet your aim or is another experiment required? Is there more related science that can be done to improve our understanding of this topic?* This is important for scientists as it allows other people to contribute and develop knowledge. It's a good place where you can get creative, imagine what you could do if you had an unlimited budget or more specialised apparatus! Giving clues as to the limitations of our findings and possible next steps are the way that scientists build on each other's findings to improve our understanding of the Universe. And that's the aim of Physics!

Choosing the Right Content

If a video covered all of these points it would be very long, and some of this stuff might not be as relevant for some experiments as it is for others. At the same time though this isn't an exhaustive list of all that you can consider in a lab report of a practical. Using these headings provides a very good frame for thinking through experimental procedures and results, do this for every experiment in your course and thinking this way becomes a habit. It is what science is, it is a process that you should enjoy, and it is the process that most exam questions are based around!

6 Make a timeline of the history of our understanding of light, include key experiments and the changes that were made to the models we use to explain the behaviour of light.

The Quantum Frontier

Quantum was the main work of physicists of the 20th Century. It seemed to be the most likely route to the *grand unifying theory* that Einstein had wanted to reach. Unification was the quest for theoretical physicists and experimental physicists alike. It was the work that culminated in the verification of the Higgs Boson by the ALICE and ATLAS experiments at CERN, by which time it had become clear that the next frontier would be a new physics that quantum mechanics would not be able to explain! Quantum was an excellent model, which fitted with evidence for a large number of observations, from macroscopic to microscopic and to the seemingly fundamental. The story of the development of our understanding of light is the story of the development of this theory of quantum mechanics.

For you learning quantum mechanics for the first time there are many points where you might have to take a leap of faith, to take the teacher or textbook at their word. In Einsteinian physics it's a good policy not to wonder why something is, but to accept that it is so. You sometimes have to accept that the evidence and the maths dictate that it *is* so. Learn to apply the theory, work through the algebra and what we call *understanding* follows.

Our models of thinking, through stories and analogy, are only as useful as far as they explain evidence. Each model has its limitations. A good teacher will take the time to explain quantum in a variety of different ways, perhaps talking about potential wells and the analogy to gravitational potential energy or likening it to the firm ideas that you likely have about electron shells from chemistry. But models and analogies create the risk of misconceptions arising and the best advice is to get your head around the evidence as it is presented to you through demonstration and experiment.

Richard Feynman, the physicist who perhaps did most to explain quantum mechanics, famously stated in his lecture series the *Character of Physical Law*: "If you think you understand quantum mechanics, you don't understand quantum mechanics." So, don't panic and take my advice; make sure you can solve the problems that they are going to give you in A Level Physics and be satisfied with this as your *understanding* of quantum. As you do more and more of these problems, you'll feel more comfortable with the terminology and the phenomena and you'll feel like you understand it just fine. Feynman's lectures can all be read online and many, including the series the *Character of Physical Law* are even available in glorious 360p black and white on YouTube! Enjoy!

Quantum Basics

In GCSE in Physics or Combined Science there was a section on energy in and out of atoms; the idea that light is a photon and it causes electrons to move between fixed energy levels in an atom. That is quantum at its most basic level; photons (light particles) are absorbed by atoms when an electron moves up energy levels, and photons are emitted from atoms when electrons move down between the fixed energy levels. The energy of the photon is equal to the discrete energy change that the electron made, and that energy is proportional to the frequency of the photon.

Also in GCSE was the electromagnetic spectrum and the idea that one end is the high frequency and therefore high energy end. A gamma photon is much higher energy than a radio photon. There were also emission and absorption spectra, discrete bands shown on spectrums where either a fixed frequency of light has been absorbed or emitted.

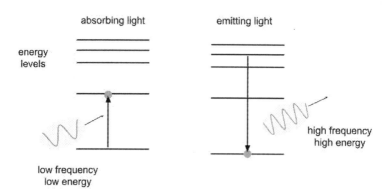

For me the first lightbulb moment with quantum was when I realised why you only see two discrete colours in a match flame, blue and orange. Soon I realised why copper compounds burn a different colour to carbon ones, and why fluorescent light bulbs give a very different emission spectrum to an incandescent light bulb. But it's really when you measure Planck's constant using the emission of light from LEDs, or by measuring the stopping voltage needed to reduce the current on a photocell to zero, that you'll *understand* quantum mechanics.

The History of Our Model of Light

This task should get you up to speed with wat happened in Physics for us to reach the point we are at now in our understanding of light. Put yourself in the mind of a pre-1600 student, and imagine you know basically nothing about light except that it travels in straight lines, and can be transmitted, absorbed or reflected, and take yourself through the voyage of discovery, this fascinating history. By bringing yourself through the debate, to our current model for light you'll have a deeper knowledge of that model and also a deeper understanding of how evidence changes models.

There's a lot written about the history of the theory of light, so I don't want to give too much away in terms of directing your research. Use your textbooks and revision guides as a first port of call to give you an idea on what to include and embellish these with extra internet and library research. Make sure you touch upon these scientists and their experiments or theories along the way; Newton, Huygens, Young, Planck and Einstein.

You could start by asking yourself; *does the evidence in each of these diagrams support a wave, or a particle theory of light, or both?*

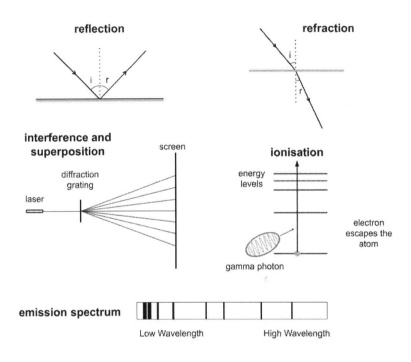

7 Review a set of AS exam papers for your course using the examiners' report to ensure that you learn from common mistakes that students make.

Warning! Be Honest with Yourself!

I strongly suggest you do this before any mock exams that your school run. However, I do recommend making sure that you don't do whichever exam paper your school is going to use as a mock exam! Generally, the older papers are less likely to be used, but if you are worried ask your teacher if you shouldn't do a certain set of papers. For this task you need to pick one that was sat as an exam, and make sure that you have access to the papers, mark schemes and examiners reports for it.

Getting the Most Out of Past Papers

I want you to use a set of exam papers in a certain way.   There are essentially 6 hours of study to be done with every exam paper, which means this task will take you 12 hours. 12 hours of the most useful study that you will do this year!

For each exam paper:

2 hours – sit the exam paper on your own, in exam conditions, be disciplined and don't be tempted to cheat. We want to find out what you can and can't do.

2 hours – mark the exam paper with the mark scheme and make corrections. As you make corrections use your textbook or revision guide to ensure that you are finding out what you should know to allow you to solve the problems in questions like this in the future. Make a note of any gaps in your knowledge and understanding to revise later.

2 hours – review the exam paper with the examiners' report. This is the best insight into why some questions are harder than others and why many people get caught out with certain types of questions. It'll help you know

exactly what command words tell you about what is required in the answers and it will provide some of the most useful study tips. Look out for the times when you get something wrong which most people get right, these should be absolute priorities to make sure you work on before your mock exams and for the real things. Look out for the times when you get something right that most people get wrong, give yourself a pat on the back at these points and know these are your strengths! Pay careful attention to the summaries, as these will give you insight into the types of things examiners will be including in the next set of exams.

Follow this method every time you study an exam paper. It is a full day of study on one exam paper, but it is the most useful way to prepare yourself for exams. Don't just study exam papers though, many students make these too large a proportion of their study time. The real use of exam papers is to check the quality and impact of the other study activities that you are doing.

8 Measure the specific heat capacity of water at home using an electric kettle.

Super Quick Methods to Measure SHC for Water

I've developed this idea from a tweet by Lewis Mattheson, of the great *GCSE and A Level Physics Online* channel, and the awesome people at the *Physics Teaching Podcast, (TP)²*. I've adapted it though because it's a good example of where we can use graphs to get greater accuracy in our experiments.

In their tweet they asked everybody to fill their kettle, making a note volume of water, hence the mass of water, m, (one litre water is equal to one kilogram of water,) then to time how long it takes for the kettle to boil, t. By making an assumption about the starting temperature of water, or if possible, measuring it, calculate the temperature change, ΔT. Each person also needed to read the power rating, P, of the kettle they were using and calculate energy supplied using $E = Pt$. And then to use the data to calculate specific heat capacity, c, using the equation $c = \frac{\Delta E}{m \Delta T}$.

In this way they were able to get a large number of specific heat capacities and to calculate an arithmetic mean. My suggestion of improvement to this would be to vary the volume of water in the kettle, and hence be able to plot a graph of mass versus energy supplied for a fixed temperature change. Try it! All you need is a measuring jug, a standard electric kettle and a stopwatch. If you do have access to accurate thermometer then brilliant, if not presume the water coming out the tap is about 15°C, (it might be a little higher or lower depending on the weather outside.)

Collect results in a table like this below, process your data using a spreadsheet, plot E on the y-axis and $m\Delta T$ on the x-axis, use a gradient to calculate specific heat capacity, and calculate a percentage difference from the accepted value of specific heat capacity of water of $4\ 200\ Jkg^{-1}K^{-1}$.

mass (kg)	time (s)	energy (J)

The benefit of using a gradient rather than an arithmetic mean is that it is influenced less by anomalies. Gradients also often limit the impact of systematic errors as this can have the effect of changing the y-intercept and not the gradient.

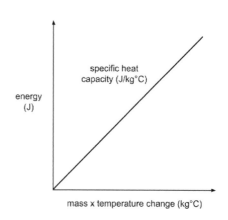

In this case though there is one systematic error which graphs will not help with. Almost every time we measure a specific heat capacity, we get a value which is a little too high, rarely is our calculated value too small. *Can you use what you know about energy stores and transfers to figure out why measured specific heat capacities are almost always higher than the true value?*

9 Measure the angular diameter of the sun and the moon using a pinhole camera

Amateur Astronomy

My neighbour has just bought a telescope, and it's amazing seeing the surface of the Moon with its craters in sharp focus. But it really blows your mind when you see Jupiter, with the pastel coloured banding and the four Galilean moons in a plane around it. If you are at all interested; get one. Most basic, inexpensive telescopes can get fantastic views of the moon, and on a clear night let you see the two largest gas giants, Jupiter and Saturn.

In this task you will not need to spend any money to make some accurate observations of celestial bodies in of our solar system. In this experiment you are going to make a pinhole camera and use it to measure the diameter of the Sun and the Moon. The value for diameter of the sun that I measured at home by following this method is $1.8 \times 10^9 m$ which is around 30% different from the true, or accepted, value of the diameter of the sun. I challenge you to be more accurate, let me know how you do.

Make a Pinhole Camera

Making a pinhole camera is easy, and there are plenty of how to videos or other webpages online if you get stuck. Basically, find a card tube, a popular crisp brand or something that bottles come in would be fine, or even roll yourself one

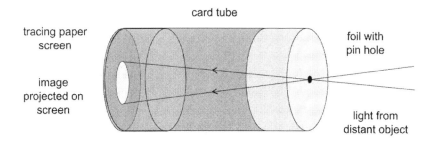

using an A4 piece of card. Either cover one end with foil, (or use the existing covered end,) and make a small hole, you can use a pin, or a cocktail stick, bamboo skewer, anything really. Don't worry about the size of the hole; the smaller it is, the sharper your image will be, but the smaller it is the darker it will be. Start small and you can always make it wider if your image is too faint to be seen. On the other end firmly and tightly tape (or attach with an elastic band) some tracing paper across it to act as the screen. If you do not have tracing paper thin printer paper will do just fine or otherwise grease-proof paper will probably work. Test out your pinhole camera by pointing it at a light bulb, or a bright window, you should be able to make out an image on your screen.

Remember never to look directly at the sun! Our eyes have their most sensitive light detecting cells at the centre of the retina, the macula, when we bring something into sharp focus, we use this part of our retina, the sun's light is intense enough to damage these cells.

You'll need a cloudless view to form images of the sun, and you'll need a clear night with a full, or nearly full moon to form images of the moon. Point your pinhole camera at the Sun or Moon so that you see a circular image of the object form on the tracing paper screen. Use a pencil or a felt tip pen (with as fine a point as possible for accuracy) to mark out the circle of the image formed on the screen of the sun. Take the paper off and measure the diameter, h_i, of the image using a ruler, take a pair of readings of the diameter and calculate an average for accuracy. Repeat if possible. Also measure also the length of your pinhole camera, v, from pinhole to screen using a ruler. Convert both values into metres, these are all the values that you need to measure.

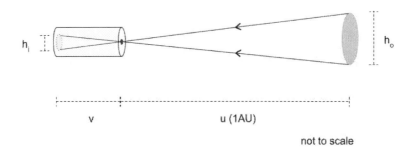

not to scale

Follow this algebra to calculate the diameter of the sun from your measured values.

you may remember this equation from GCSE, or at least you'll have the idea of an image being magnified or diminished, this equation states that the magnification m is a scale factor equal to the ratio of the image height, h_i, over the object height, h_o

$$m = \frac{h_i}{h_o} \qquad (1)$$

we can also define magnification as the ratio of the distance from the pinhole (or normally optical centre of a lens,) v, to the object and the distance from the pinhole to the object, u

$$m = \frac{v}{u} \qquad (2)$$

make the two equations for magnification equal

$$\frac{h_i}{h_o} = \frac{v}{u} \qquad (3)$$

and rearrange for object height and we have an equation for the height of the object

$$h_o = \frac{h_i u}{v} \qquad (4)$$

In this case the distance, u, from the pinhole to the sun is one astronomical unit, 1AU, the distance between Earth and the Sun, $1.50 \times 10^{11} m$. The image height is your measured diameter of your image.

Once you've done the maths, firstly marvel at just how big the sun is and then leave a comment somewhere on GorillaPhysics YouTube channel to let me know how close your measured value was to the true value!

10 Make a flowchart of the development of key theories in astrophysics. Try to include how each astronomer builds upon the theories that came before them.

We all love learning about space! Take some time, probably during a holiday, over this one. Use internet research, your textbooks, revision guides and YouTube to create a flowchart of key theories in astrophysics.

It is true that not all of these themes will be in your A Level, but do not let that stop you the aim of this task is to help you get some enthusiasm and motivation for the challenge ahead, you'll need it when it gets hard. It's fascinating to see how your study fits in with the development of ideas and theories throughout time so far and into the future. Also, the theme of evidence changing theory is a key idea in all science qualifications. I have written the ones that are most likely to be relevant to your A Level in bold.

- Primitive Man & Early Civilisations

- Ancient Greeks

- Copernicus

- Tycho Brahe

- **Kepler**

- **Galileo**

- **Newton**

- Moon's Acceleration

- Planetary Motion

- Masses of Sun and Jupiter

- Comet

- Tides

- Mass of the Moon

- Irregularities in the Motion of the Moon

- Bulge of Earth

- Progression of Equinoxes

- Perturbations of Planets

- Einstein's Theory of Gravity

- **Hubble and the Expanding Universe**

- The Space Race

- Cosmic Microwave Background Radiation

- **The Cosmological Principle**

- **Cosmic Distance Ladder – How we measure distance in the Universe**

- **Stellar Classification and Evolution – Wein's Law / Stefan's Law and Hertzsprung-Russel Diagrams**

- **Swarzchild Radius**

- Exploring our Solar System

- **Neutron Stars**

- Pulsars

- **Black Holes**

- Hubble Telescope and the Deep Field Image

- Large Scale Structure

- **Critical Density and the Ultimate Fate of the Universe?**

- Dark Matter and Dark Energy

Pro-tip: Knowing more than just what's on your specification is a great way to prepare yourself for the hardest questions. If you are aiming for the A* you need to be reading widely around the subject!
Having a broad bank of physics contexts is useful for developing the skill of applying your subject content knowledge to the novel contexts that they will give you in exam questions.
See independent task 13 for more on this!

---

11 Conduct your own practical at home into Coulomb's Law using kitchen scales, a balloon and a packet of crisps.

Coulomb's Law

Coulomb's Law relates the force between charged objects, F, to the distance between them, r. It's an inverse square law so that means the force is proportional to 1 over the distance between objects squared; $F \propto \frac{1}{r^2}$. It's difficult to accurately measure quantities like force and charge with static electricity but we can observe some of the effects of Coulomb's Law by simple experiments like the one in this task.

Coulomb's law can be written as:

$$F = \frac{kQ_1Q_2}{r^2} \qquad \text{where} \qquad k = \frac{1}{4\pi\varepsilon_0}$$

ε_0 is the permittivity of free space and has the value $8.85 \times 10^{-12} Fm^{-1}$. Q_1 and Q_2 are the charges of the two objects in Coulombs.

Practice using equations to give definitions. In a question like *state what is meant by Coulomb's law.* You could write the equation as a sentence, as an answer. *The force between two charged objects is proportional to the product of their charges and inversely proportional to the square of the distance between them.*

Equilibrium

To start try this simple demo. Get two balloons and inflate them. Tie a string to the knotted end of each balloon. Charge of balloons by rubbing them on your hair or on a woollen jumper or other insulating material. Hold the two balloons by the middle of the string out at arm's length and think about what you notice. Hopefully you can get them to be held apart for a period of time, just as in this diagram.

This is a common situation that is used in exam questions, and it combines what you know about forces in equilibrium with your understanding of Coulomb's law. In the example in the image two spheres on strings are held apart by the electrostatic force, *F.* They may tell you the mass of the spheres, the tension in the strings, *T,* the angle that they are held

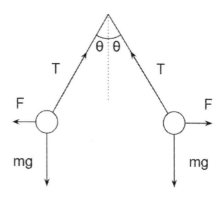

apart and the distance between them at equilibrium, *θ*. From this you can work out the size of the repulsive force and using Coulomb's law work back to the charges on the spheres.

Experiment

Here's an amazing experiment you can do at home to confirm the inverse square relationship in Coulomb's law. We need a way to measure force and distance. We are not going to be able to measure charge at home, but we can assume that it will be constant for short periods of time.

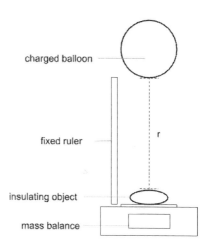

One way to measure force is to use a top pan balance. You probably have one of these in your kitchen. Go ahead and eat a packet of crisps, and then roll up the crisp packet into a small triangle, I'm sure there'll be numerous videos on how to do this somewhere online. You could use any insulator, but a packet of crisps is something I've seen it work well with.

Figure out a way to measure distance, for example by fixing a ruler behind the top pan balance. You are going to take a short video clip as you bring the charged balloon towards the crisp packet, making sure you can see the reading on top and balance and the ruler scale.

Charge your balloon by rubbing on your jumper or hair, then bring it from a distance of around half a metre towards the crisp packet on the balance, videoing on your phone as you go. Be careful to avoid parallax by trying to make sure your camera is always at 90 degrees to the ruler and make sure that you don't touch the balloon against anything else, as that will discharge it. Watch your video back and decide if you need to repeat the experiment or if you feel you have a quality set of results.

Analysis

Analyse your results by reading pairs of values for distance and mass on the balance, try and get about ten data points. Input these into a spreadsheet. You can convert the mass, which is likely in grams from the balance, into kg and then into newtons if by multiplying by 9.81ms^{-2} (or you could just be happy to say that mass is proportional to the force on the crisp packet.) Plot a graph, distance on the x-axis and force on the y axis. You should be able to fit an inverse square curve by using polynomial trendline in excel, look at the power of x in the equation, it should be close to -2.

Then make a second table with your force values in one column and $\frac{1}{r^2}$ in the second column. Plot these you should find a straight line through the origin. This is evidence for the relationship proposed by Coulomb's law.

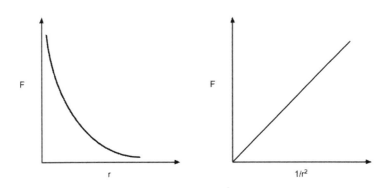

12 Turn one of your PAG lab reports into an academic poster. Think through the criticisms that someone could make of your experiment and address them. Make sure you include all the details that they may ask you about in the exams!

Academic Research Posters

When scientific research is published the researchers always make a poster. These are not attention-grabbing adverts for their research, they are large landscape presentations of their methodologies, results and conclusions. They are designed to be put up at conferences, to be presented to delegates as they walk through a conference floor, for people to use as focus of discussion around the merits of the research. After a conference the posters are usually put up in the corridors of the research institution for visitors and other researchers to digest the research in a more casual way.

You are going to make an academic poster of your own. This could form a part of a display for one of your classrooms, or as part of an open evening display to encourage other people to follow your lead and take up the challenge of A Level Physics. I suggest that you work as part of a group for this one.

Before you start search do an image search of *scientific research poster* to give you an understanding of how these things are presented. I've given an example from a group of my students on the next page. Perhaps also do a website search on what to include in a scientific research poster. They usually have their graphs and summary data presented at the centre of the sheet and blocks of writing, using subheadings (like those we used in task 5) to make key details accessible more rapidly, on either side. Your goals will be different to University students and graduates presenting their work, but this task is meant to give you an idea of the challenges associated with presenting your work in this way. Find the official exam board instructions sheets and watch YouTube videos of the experiment to help you.

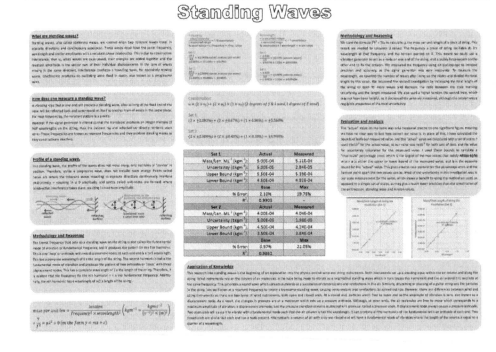

Choosing the Right Content

In an academic poster you don't need to include everything, for example you do not need your entire set of raw results as you should in a full lab report. You do not need your full method or all your calculations. This is a process of selecting the most relevant and most important information from your lab report that you've already made. Choose the most evaluative comments, choose the most relevant and concise writing that you have done and present this. Summarise your experiment is a formal but attractive way. Careful selection of material is an important skill for further study or the world of work, so take the time to enjoy and see the relevance of doing this.

In doing this hopefully you will get to know this particular experiment in a really deep and meaningful way, and this will be invaluable experience when you come to summarise all of the practicals in your course in flashcard form in one of the later tasks.

13 Use IFL science to design your own questions based in unfamiliar contexts, and so get used to applying your subject knowledge to new contexts in exam situations. https://www.iflscience.com/physics/

Why Students Don't Get Questions

Every A Level student I have met has had the same complaint about exams. They say something along the lines of, "I know it, I get it, but they start the question with some weird context and I've no idea what the question is even about." Yep, that's the issue most students face as they move up from GCSE to A Level.

The students that end up getting the top grades are the ones that have a plan on how to deal with it! This task will give you a way to deal with it.

Understanding challenge lies in understanding that examinations in this country are all based around something called Bloom's taxonomy, which is a hierarchy of skills. I hope you'll have seen it in your lessons, it's normally presented as a little pyramid and has the skills from easiest but most common at the bottom to hardest and least common at the top. Look up the assessment objectives for A Level sciences and you will see these words embedded in them!

The skills are, from least difficult to most; knowledge, understanding, application, analysis, evaluation and creativity. Creativity exists in its own little world, but the rest you will find exactly, in that order, in the assessment objectives, which is what the government say exam boards must test in exams.

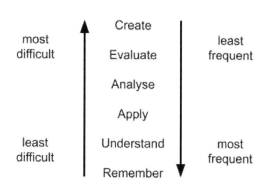

I talk about this idea of taxonomy for exams in my popular *Do These 4 Things to Get an A* in A Level Physics* video. https://youtu.be/r7i1-9csYnI

It's good news that the thing most people struggle with, applying knowledge, is not the very hardest skill! And just like any other skill it takes practice. If you practice applying your knowledge and understanding to unfamiliar contexts, you'll be better at it in exams, you'll be more resilient and get in less of a panic during the stressful exam situation. In fact, once you've really worked on this skill, you'll notice that the vast majority of describe and explain questions can be completed without reading any of the context contained in the stem of the question at all!

How to Write Hard Questions

In this task put yourself in the shoes of the examiner and write some of the most difficult questions you can manage. Start with a tricky context and write a range of questions which draw out the examination *content* from that *context*.

I like the website IFL Science as a source of ideas because the writing is very accessible and interesting. Go there and read a few articles. As you read think to yourself: *What areas of the A Level Physics course could I apply to this context?* In doing this you are already practicing the skill of application, and you'll be better at thinking to yourself in the exam: *What area of the course can I apply to this question?*

Once you've picked an article, write a few easier questions. Write the parts first, so for example: *a. Describe the …. b. Explain how…. c. Calculate the….* Then write the stem of the question, that is a short bit of information from the article that you read. Think if there is any useful information that you can provide which might give clues to the student answering the question, as to the content that they need to apply. Add any data that they might need for calculation or to reference in a *conclude* or *justify* question. Try and work through the taxonomy, thinking about those assessment objectives as you do so to help you think up some of the hardest questions. Write a really hard question using analytical or evaluative skills but try to ensure that there is enough detail in the question and the stem such that the response that you are after is unambiguous. Look back at past exam questions to see how they give clues to the response that they expect in the way they write the questions, and in what they include, or choose to leave out of the exam question.

It's a good idea to find a list of the command words that your exam board uses and what exactly they mean, they are usually in the specification or are very prominent on the course page on the exam board's website.

Lastly write yourself a mark scheme, including all the possible responses that you feel will be worthy of credit, and maybe excluding a few responses which do not meet the level of answer that you are expecting from your question. Print your question out and challenge your friends and classmates, and maybe even your teacher, to answer your question.

I suggest that you do this a few times over your course. Think carefully about this experience, of what goes into a difficult but unambiguous *apply* exam question. I promise you; exam questions are not weird and wonderful, they are not difficult to decode or decipher and the examiner is not trying to catch you out. Questions are specific, written in plain English and give plenty of indication of the type of response that they are expecting.

Examiners write questions that have challenge at all levels, so in each question there will be parts which are just simple recall, some parts which you must demonstrate your understanding, and some parts which are much harder than that. Remember in the exam you can always pick up the easier marks in a question so long as you don't get put off by the tricky context that the examiner has come up with! It's just a matter of practicing the skill of recognising the subject content within the context of the question.

Pro-tip: You must take your revision further than just trying to memorise content. Recalling content verbatim is an important part of the A Level, but it is a much smaller part than it was at GCSE. You need to not only make sure you know all the stuff, but that you can do all the skills. Do not ignore these skills when you go through checklists and specifications when planning your priorities for revision.

Doing plenty of exam questions will also help you develop your skills.

14 Make a timeline of the key discoveries in particle physics. Give details of the experiments that were conducted and relate the evidence to the particle or property being investigated.

Particle Physics is a story of theory and experiment. Theoretical physicists predict using mathematical arguments and experimental physicists design experiments to verify, or *discover,* those particles the theory predicts. It is not the case that any of these particles were stumbled upon, the theory told experimenters where to look!

Use research to make a timeline of the key *discoveries* in particle Physics. Make sure that you are focussed on the ones that are important for your specification, but don't be scared to extend beyond the textbook as this fascinating area will give you lots to be enthusiastic about and that will motivate you through the hard study to come.

Here are some headings which are in most specifications to get you started:

- JJ Thompson's discovery of the electron
- Rutherford's alpha particle scattering experiment
- Einstein's explanation of the photo electric effect
- Chadwick's discovery of the neutron
- Gell-Mann's deep inelastic scatting experiment
- the four fundamental forces
- discoveries of subsequent generations of matter
- conservation laws in particle physics
- development of the Standard Model
- the discovery of the Higgs Boson
- what's next in particle physics

15 Answer the question: *which book had more impact, Isaac Newton's Principles of Mathematics or Einstein's Special and General Theory of Relativity?*

The Two Books

One theory which General Relativity replaced is Newton's Law of Universal Gravitation. It is not that Newton's Law was wrong, but General Relativity holds true for more situations than Newton's Law does. It is currently our best explanation of gravity, and recently the gravitational waves predicted by it have been observed at LIGO, the Laser Interferometer Gravitational-Wave Observatory. However, this task is not about whose ideas are more correct, or who was the bigger genius; it is about which book had more impact.

This will not be an easy task. If you are not careful you will get into an endlessly descriptive mode of writing in trying to answer this question. Instead you need to find a way to evaluate the impact of the two books.

Both books are era-defining. They encapsulate a new thinking in Physics. It is reductive to say, but Newton's book brought about the use of calculus to analyse physical evidence and Einstein's book brought about the use of the reference frame for considering relativistic effects. Both contain laws that are still accepted and repeatedly evidenced today. Both books are undoubtedly the work of genius. But which influenced what came next the most.

I am not expecting you to read both, although both can be found as PDFs or transcripts for free online with just a limited amount of digging. You may well need to write a short summary, maybe just a set of bullet points indicating briefly what each contains. You may like to read some of it, find excerpts or just pick a few pages and give them a go, just to get a flavour of what the writing is like. But don't spend ages trying to get your head around their ideas expressed in their words, this is not an English exercise, where it might well be important to analyse the linguistic modes of the authors, it is enough to know an outline of the physics ideas the books present.

Focus Your Ideas

Ask yourself these types of questions:

- What can we do now as a result of these theories?
- Who else quotes these books as major influences in their work?
- What practical uses have we found for these theories and laws?
- How were these books received by the writers' contemporaries?
- Were they criticised or largely accepted?
- How often are they quoted or referenced in other work?
- How many people have read them?

You might even come up with some sort of scoring system, whereby you can assess the importance of the books against a range of criteria; or you might just wish to treat the matter qualitatively. You might just focus on one important thing which came about as a result of these books. There are no right answers to this task and I'm looking forward to seeing what you come up with as an answer to this quite nebulous question!

Some Ideas

We define just about everything that comes after Newton and before Einstein as *Newtonian Physics*. *Newtonian Physics* is Physics which can be explained mathematically, by reduction of phenomena to proportional relationships. Newton's Universe can be modelled by applying reason and theories can be treated empirically.

Everything changed after Einstein's miracle year. In one year he wrote *Special Relativity*, explained Brownian motion, elegantly quantised light in his Photoelectric Equation, and gave the world a way to unlock vast amounts of energy in his equation $E = mc^2$. Everything from then on, we term *Einsteinian Physics*. It's another epoch for Physics, where suddenly the start point for every question, every hypothesis, needs to be *which frame of reference are we working in?*

The distinction between classical and relativistic treatment of phenomena is not something you have to do much of in A Level Physics, but there are plenty of Einsteinian ideas which you will have to apply. The annihilation of matter and antimatter, calculating the energy released in nuclear reactions and the relativistic effects as a particle approaches the speed of light are a notable few.

This task is a designed to be a taste of what comes next if you take your study to the next level. We are now at the start of a new era of Physics that was started with the discovery of the Higgs Boson. It is a task in which you will need to think evaluatively, and this will help you think evaluatively when you read texts at University, texts which may come to define the start of the next era of Physics.

16 Annotate your Equation Sheet with extra details and instructions on how or when to use each equation or piece of data. This simple technique will help your memory under pressure in the exam!

Ebbinghaus System and Location Based Memory

This is by far my favourite revision technique! I talk about it quite a lot on my channel because I think it is such a good idea. It combines the two most compelling theories we have about memory; the Ebbinghaus system and the method of loci. I'll chat you through those two ideas.

Ebbinghaus did a lot of research about forgetting, his conclusions were that if you learned something once and didn't revisit it then your retention of those items would decrease rapidly. His research went on to find that if you revisit the material for short periods of time after short intervals then you quickly bring yourself back up to maximum retention of the facts. Importantly in doing so you decrease the rate at which you forget. His work is often summarised into what is often called *the forgetting curve*. (The graph presented on the next page.)

This is the evidence for the repeated and spaced pattern of revision that your teachers will recommend to you. You need to plan into your study time short periods of revisiting material you learned last week, two weeks ago, a month

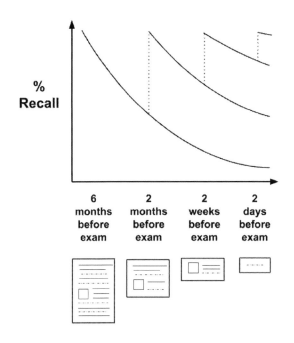

ago, last term etc. Each time you do this you put that memory deeper and deeper into your long-term memory. This is why schools have so many topic tests and mock exams planned into the year, to kind of remind you, (or to force you), to go through this process of revisiting old material.

Also there isn't time to go over the material in the exact same way as we learned it in the first time, so we use summaries. Repeated learning might go something like this; *first learning*, an hour long lesson on a topic; *second learning*, summarise your notes from the lesson onto one A4 sheet; *third learning*, summarise the sheet onto one flashcard or one paragraph; *fourth learning*, reduce the notes to a set of key words or bullet points. Each time we summarise and reduce our learning we revisit the last more detailed version, and those details embed themselves into our deeper memory. Summarising material is also a high-level task, where you are having to evaluate and select material to include or exclude, it is in itself a valuable learning activity.

The second most compelling theory of memory is that of the method of loci, that is using location to enhance memory. This is by no means a modern technique; it was used by the ancient Greeks and Romans! When Sherlock Holmes wants to recall a certain fact about criminology or forensics, he goes into his *mind palace*; a great house that he has constructed in his brain with rooms for topic, and furniture in each room containing the detail. The point is that we Humans have excellent spatial memory, (probably evolved to enable us to be better hunter-gatherers, or to help us find our way home, or avoid dangers,) and that if we place a fact in a particular place we are more likely to be able to recall it. Teachers use this all the time; it is one reason for us using seating plans, I can honestly remember the names of entire classes that I taught ten years ago by imagining my classroom at the time and thinking about where each student sat! However, if I bump into those young people in the street, I'm often at a loss for their names! It's the same reason you'll find it easier to remember quotes in an English classroom and Physics equations in a science classroom! And I would recommend this, if it is at all possible in your school; go into your exam hall with all your notes, sit in the chair you expect to sit at and place those memorisation items in various locations around the room!

Synthesis

This task combines the two methods of memory enhancement; summarising, reducing and revisiting, and using locations to organise your memories. Take an equation sheet exactly like you'll be given in your exam, and work through it with your revision guide or notes, adding topic detail next to the equations for each topic. Add things that you think you'll forget, add units, sketch graphs, diagrams, common explain answers, definitions of key terms, common clues as to when to use each equation, details about experiments; add any details that you think are important. Use this annotated equation sheet in all your lessons rather than using a blank one. Keep adding any detail as you learn more, or as you identify more bits you need to memorise. Then, when it is time to do another mock exam take a new blank sheet and your annotated sheet and reduce the notes on it. Maybe now you think you'll not have any trouble remembering this fact or that fact, so you can leave them off, or summarise them in fewer words.

Repeat this reduction and refinement of your annotated equation sheet until during the exam season you have such a good memory of that detail that you put onto the sheet that you can take a blank equation sheet and remember exactly what you wrote here, or there, next to that equation or under that heading. Use these sheets every time you do a past paper or do summary questions. I assure you your memory will improve in this way! Give it a try, you will not regret it.

17 Review last year's exam papers using the examiner's report, make sure you are aware of the attributes that distinguish a higher-level response from a weaker response.

Sit Papers – Mark – Review

You completed an exam paper review exercise earlier in task 7, where you reviewed a set of AS papers. Now it is time to do the same for full A Level papers.

There's a lot of past papers, every A Level has around 6 hours of exams! It is well worth planning each of these exercises into a week where you know you'll have plenty of time. Make this task a priority and do it thoroughly.

Use last year's exam papers, mark schemes and reports, (they are normally released to all around Easter, but if not, ask your teachers for them.) Do the exam in timed conditions, mark it thoroughly and harshly with the mark schemes, and then review each question with the examiners' report. Pay close attention to the suggestions the examiners make.

Learn About Yourself from Other People's Mistakes

You may have done the previous year's papers as mock exams, in which case it's perfect, you can go straight to the examiners reports and really look carefully at the reasons why you did or didn't get the marks. If you haven't already done them then do the exams in quiet, timed conditions, getting rid of any distractions like mobile phones, music or TV. Use it to gauge your time management for the real thing, and practice using spare time to check back with the command words and other clues in the questions and check the algebra and calculations again.

Find out the places where you are likely to make mistakes. For example I know that in calculations I make mistakes in three main ways; powers of ten, usually copying them wrong or putting them into the calculator wrong, getting positive and negative mixed up in vector calculations and by not having my calculator set up in degrees or radians when doing trig functions! Because I know these are *my* common errors, I always check them after calculations.

Don't Give Yourself the Benefit of the Doubt (BOD Marks)

Be harsh with the mark schemes, there is no mark given for *yeah, that's what I meant*, we do expect answers in the terms given on the mark scheme. Examiners are really specific about what they do or do not allow, don't presume one word is equivalent to another; *linear* is not the same as *directly proportional, vibration* is not the same as *oscillation, potential difference* is not the same as *EMF, threshold frequency* is not the same as *work function…* there are many more examples of common mix-ups that students make! In these cases, the student has the right idea, but uses the wrong words. They get it, but they just haven't used the correct terms for the marks. So be harsh on yourself when you mark your own work! Examiners are strict with the mark scheme because it makes our marking consistent and fair. Besides, this is just practice, and the more exactly you follow a mark scheme the better you'll be in the real thing!

Personally, I think that there isn't much point trying to predict what will come up in exam papers based on the previous years, as with any guess work sometimes you'll be right, sometimes wrong. But I do think it's worth knowing what is in the mind of the examiners in terms of their priorities for students to be learning. Luckily for us they set out these priorities in the examiners' reports, they make it clear in fact. These documents are intended for teachers, but they are perfect for those of you that are aiming for the top grades. They'll help you to get into the mindset of the examiners and find out what responses they are expecting from each type of question. They'll also help you to see common errors that you are perhaps guilty of as well, and in knowing them, you're more likely to spot them yourself in the exam and avoid them.

Pro-tip: The examiners' reports are the most useful document in preparing for exams! Use them to make sure you don't make the common errors from previous years!

18 Review all of the core practicals, required practicals or PAGs in your specification and ensure that you have complete notes for each practical.

Reduce Notes

Here's where it was so useful to be making complete, detailed lab reports of the experiments as you conducted them throughout the course. This revision technique is about reduction. Reduction of detailed notes into summaries is one of the memorisation techniques which came out of the research of Ebbinghaus, which you met in task 16. It will help you memorise all the details about all the important experiments that you have conducted in your course.

Reduce the detailed lab reports into summary notes or cards for each practical. Just cover these headings below and focus on the specific details given in the official exam board practical guide. If you haven't done every practical specified in your course then you can still use the practical guide to write summaries of the key details you need to know for the exams, (you only need to have done a minimum of 12 for your CPAC qualification).

You might even add in some of the experiments that you have learned about, that you will definitely not have been able to do. Exam questions are often based around key experiments in Physics, so knowing the details of, for example; Rutherford's alpha particle scattering, Millikan's oil drop experiment or deep inelastic scattering, might be a massive help!

Select Key Details

This activity is about knowing the experiments in the exact way that they are specified by the exam board as that is the form that they will be presented to you in the questions in the exams.

Make notes on:

Equipment – *What exact apparatus are specified in this experiment? Are there several options which may impact the method or the accuracy of the outcome?* Make sure to give details on the resolution or dimensions of the apparatus and make sure you know why each piece of apparatus is suitable for each measurement. For example, a micrometer has a resolution of 0.01mm but have a range 0-25mm, it cannot be used to measure objects larger than two and a half centimetres!

Procedure – *What are the accurate techniques that we are always going to use when we measure the quantities in the experiment?* Make sure that you justify why you are using a certain technique. For example; when we time an oscillation of a period less than a few seconds, we use a fiducial marker (timing marker) and time for ten full swings, and divide by ten, this is because our expected uncertainty due to our reaction time is a significant percentage of the time period, by dividing by ten we have also reduced that percentage uncertainty by a factor of 10!

Improvements – *What are the common ways that we can improve upon practical results or method?* Make a note of the *specific* improvements for each practical. For example, repeating measurements do not always lead to more accuracy; for example, in electrical experiments we do not repeat measurements as this can lead to heating of the circuit components and therefore alter the result. Also, where there is a systematic error, repeated measurements will not lead to a mean which is closer to the true value, this improvement is only valid for random errors. Most improvements will be centred around the idea of minimising percentage uncertainty, so think of ways to either reduce the absolute uncertainty of the measurement or to increase the value of the quantity you are measuring.

Mathematical Models – *What is the analysis that you must do in the experiment to get the final result? What graphs do you plot? How do you manipulate the algebra so that you get a graph in the form $y = mx + c$? What does the gradient and the y-intercept represent in each case?* Going through this thinking also ensures that you appreciate which variables need to be changed, measured and kept constant in the practical.

If it helps, I made a run through of all the experiments in three A Level Courses, I'd recommend watching them all regardless of your exam board as they all use the same list of apparatus and techniques and sometimes knowing alternative methods can help you be resilient when they give you variations on the specified methods in your course:

Every Core Practical in A Level Physics (Edexcel): https://youtu.be/Ip8cenhaY1Q

Every AQA A Level Physics Required Practical: https://youtu.be/NrLCP1WlyD4

All the OCR A Level Physics PAGs: https://youtu.be/TaGxKw4IsgU

These videos are good because I also go through what is expected in the questions that they ask you around the experiments.

Knowing these details will both enable you to describe methods that you've already done and to design your own methods. Knowing the apparatus and techniques in A Level physics experiments will help you analyse results that are given to you and to evaluate methods and results of others that are presented to you in exams.

Extra Independent Tasks

Year 12

- **Make a list of every definition that you need to know in A Level Physics, these are often made bold in textbooks or identified in specifications or on checklists.**
  You cannot afford to lose marks on simple definitions! Even at A Level there are marks just for memory, that's questions that start *write, state, outline, list, describe, define* etc. Also, within longer written questions there will be marks for accurate definitions. Missing out one or two words from a definition can change its meaning enough such that it is not going to score the mark. You can use glossaries that already exist in textbooks, but you do need to learn definitions well so that you do not miss out on these easy recall marks.

- Make a list of all the laws and first principles of physics which you are expected to know and apply. These are the most important big ideas in Physics and are often the basis of exam questions.

Recognising the law or principle that a particular exam question is centred around is a really good start point for solving the problem that it poses you. Principles and Laws are the central themes in each topic of your Physics syllabus, and they will be in the forefront of the person's mind as they write your exam papers. I like this task and I've made a video about it called *A Level Laws and First Principles...* here: https://youtu.be/9LQ-m5e_Yr0

- Compare several ways of revising. Evaluate their effectiveness by reflecting on the score you got in a recent test that you studied for using a particular study technique. Discuss your thoughts with your friends and/or your teachers and try out a new study technique!

Perhaps the most important skill for study is to know when the tasks that you are doing are or are not helping you. Your teachers will help you to do this by structuring a course with lots of topic tests and mock exams, which are just little checkpoints for you to find out how well you are doing. Many students start revising for their A Levels in the same way as they revised for GCSE. Pretty soon most find out that the repetitive memory techniques, or the making of notes or flashcards, just doesn't work (on its own) at A Level.

A Level is such a massive increase in challenge from GCSE that you need to find ways of revising that are challenging, ways of revising that make sure you are working at those higher levels of taxonomy, as this is going to be the most effective use of your time.

- Review A Level Physics blogs and decide which you find the most useful.

There is lots of material available online. Many teachers share their resources in blogs, or on twitter or on YouTube. *GorillaPhysics* is just one of place where you can get free tuition to supplement your classes and your textbooks! It probably isn't the best either, I think it's got some of the highest-level learning available online, and is the best for aiming for the A*. I've got a lot more videos to make to make it more consistent and to make sure I've covered absolutely everything in the A Levels. That's my evaluation of it anyway!

Have a little search online for some of the independent teacher (or student) blogs for A Level Physics, evaluate them, and decide whether they are going to be useful resources for you. Some might be more useful for one topic and less useful at another, you might find one has great notes on the experiments but not so good for the theory sections, one might have some really challenging questions but not a lot of notes, you might find one with great animations or one with some really cool context links. Find them, evaluate them and share your thoughts with your friends and teachers. Here are a few that I found just with a simple search for *A Level Physics Blog*:

The great https://www.alevelphysicsonline.com/

Cowen Physics http://cowenphysics.com/

PhysBot http://www.physbot.co.uk/

The Comprehensive HyperPhysics http://hyperphysics.phy-astr.gsu.edu/hbase/hframe.html

Year 13

- **Make your notes into a set of flashcards and test out your friends.** The crucial part of this task is *test out your friends*! Once made, flashcards are excellent resources. But making the flashcards is not the revision activity. Don't worry about having the neatest stack of flashcards, worry about the process of making them and then memorising them. Select the key information well and then use them in creative ways to test yourself, test your friends, test your teacher and have other people test you. Make sure that you carry them with you and use them to fill little bits of time with cycling through the stack of cards. Use them, edit them, refine them, bin them when you feel that you are not going to forget them. I want to see scruffy packs of flashcards that you've spent hours messing around with, not pristine, beautifully neat colour coded cards in plastic wallets!

- **Make a list of really difficult questions and test out your teacher.**

I honestly do think writing your own questions is a valuable revision exercise. I've asked classes to do this exercise many times and I'm always really surprised at the responses that I get. The students don't seem to have much of an awareness of how exam questions are phrased, or structured. They don't seem to realise how the command word dictates the response type, and they don't regularly have a really good idea of what they are expected to be able to do according to the specification! Most of the time exam questions written by students are either too easy, or way too hard. Sometimes students leave out bits of information that you need in order to answer and other times they give away the answer to part a. when they write part b.! Of course, it is completely understandable, *why would students be able to write good quality exam questions?* They are typically written by our most experienced teachers!

Have a go at writing your own question. Try and use correct command words and think very carefully about what you do and don't state in the question. Task 13 will give you a little more detail about how to go about it. Test your teacher and your class out with them, and don't be surprised or upset when they tell you that your question isn't quite as it should be. Hopefully you'll learn a bit more about the way questions are written and it'll make it a little easier to decode them in the exam situation.

- **Make a set of cards with all the derivations that you are expected to be able to do in the exams.**

   Derivations are some of the hardest parts of A Level Physics, but in most specifications, they give you a good indication of the derivations that you are expected to be able to do in the exam. You can get a good idea by taking your specification PDF and searching for the word *derive*. Work through your textbook and make a card of each derivation that you see. I think learning these derivations by heart is a really good way to take the pressure off in the exam situation but also it is good practice for honing your skills in manipulating algebra. I have a video with all the derivations that I could find in several A Level specifications, *Derivations and Half Term Revision...* it might make a good start point: https://youtu.be/cho2iiAh7as

- **Look back over your notes for the two years of A Level Physics or use a checklist. Write a list of priorities that you need to study.**
  Honestly, students are often not honest enough with themselves about their priorities! I don't mean to be mean, or to make accusations, it's human nature to either overestimate our abilities, or underestimate them. You really need to find a way to accurately gauge your competence in the topics in A Level Physics. Doing many multiple-choice questions might give you an idea of the areas you need to prioritise, otherwise reviewing past exam papers that you have done against a list of topics might help you to identify your weaker areas. When you start your cycle of revision, for a mock exam or for the real thing, *start with the bit you find hardest,* you start with the bits you find least comfortable. It is the most common mistake, (after procrastinating or delaying,) students make with revision; to start on the most comfortable topics. It seems *logical* to think, *I'll get off to a good start and carry that positivity into the harder bits.* You should beware of logic, because what normally happens from experience is that you run out of energy and enthusiasm when it comes to the hard bits! Far better to start with the bits that you find hardest, tackle them when you've got the energy, the time and the willingness and then look forward to the sections you find most accessible once you've got some of the bits that you dread out of the way.

- **Research a current or recent experiment.**
  Now that you've studied A Level Physics, you'll be amazed at what your knowledge gives you access to. You can apply what you know to allow you to understand cutting edge Physics on more than just a basic level! Reading and thinking about how your knowledge is applied in these experiments is great revision for preparing you for those tricky apply questions in the exams! Here are some ideas of areas for research which might get you interested:
  - Find out about the *LIGO* experiment, (*the Laser Interferometer Gravitational-Wave Observatory*), which is the experiment to measure gravitational waves from distant interactions of massive objects.
  - Read about new ways to store electrical energy when there's low demand for it overnight, for example *ARES*, (*Advanced Rail Energy*

Storage) system in the United States, which eliminates the need for large chemical cells.

- Research the *LHCb* experiment (*Large Hadron Collider beauty experiment*) which is searching for the reason we live in a matter universe and not an antimatter universe, by studying the ratios in which b particles are created vs anti-b particles.
- Look into the development of hyperloops, which are train tracks within evacuated tunnels to reduce drag and make super-efficient, high speed, public transport.
- Find out about the *James Webb Space Telescope. What makes it different to the Hubble and what do we hope to find out about the universe with it?* Or just spend hours on the Hubblesite gallery, admiring our universe.
- Research the Event Horizon Telescope. *What are the benefits of making an Earth-sized telescope array? What did we learn as a result of this experiment?*

Pro-tip: You know I'm a fan of YouTube right!?
There are some amazing Physics videos out there, it's a great place to go for some really directed study, on my channel, or on loads of others. But it's also a great place to get inspired. Whenever you feel that you need some motivation to study hard don't be afraid to spend a little time watching some of the amazing YouTubers out there, popularising Physics. As you watch you can think of how the ideas that are being discussed relate to your own studies. It helps you put your knowledge in context and that just helps you be a more complete, more fluent student.
That's the aim of following the exercises in this book; to make you fluent and confident in your Physics knowledge and skills.

Most Importantly...

Get excited, get interested, think about your future, think about the challenge that is about to come your way. I always begin my classes congratulating them on having picked the most fascinating A Level, but to be aware that they have picked the most challenging.

Later in the course, when things start to get difficult, I remind my classes that they picked Physics for a reason. Either they want to go into Physics, or something Physics related, or they want to show their academic qualities, or Physics has captured their imagination and they are fascinated to be learning about the subject. You need this desire to get through the challenge of A Level Physics, so I suggest you take the time now to think about your own reasons for studying A Level and allow that enthusiasm to keep you going through those more difficult study sessions.

This book should give you many things to do to strengthen your skills as a student. The tasks are designed to stretch the most able but also to help you gain the qualities which successful A Level Physics students rely on. Believe in yourself, even when you feel that the challenge is getting too much. Be open with your teachers, family and friends when you are struggling. Remind yourself that struggling is not the same as failing, and think of how far you have come in your studies so far! You got this.

Pro-tip: Your class are an amazing resource, set up a study period at school once or twice a week and work on some key areas that you have found difficult. When you find that you all have a similar priority ask your teachers to revisit that topic. You can get some good healthy competition going as well, but remember not to feel bad if you aren't getting as high grades as others in your class. It doesn't make you a worse Physicist, just that you don't do so well under exam conditions!

Feedback is Always Welcome and Always Useful

Thanks very much for using this study guide. If you liked it and found it useful, please take the time to leave a review or to recommend it to other students or your teachers. I'd love to hear from you with any comments about it. If you didn't like it, then please tell me! Perhaps I have made a mistake somewhere, I'd love to read a correction. Perhaps my explanation of something is not very clear to you, I'd love to hear about it. Perhaps there is something else that you think would be useful for students beginning studying A Level Physics, I'd love to hear your suggestions.

Learning is a continuous process; it is not only preparation for exams, and it does not stop with the exams. Make sure that you take the feedback of your teachers seriously and with the good intent that it is meant. You <u>can</u> do this; remember this when some of your classmates do better than you in a test, or when you get a comment on your work that you think is harsh. Some people take longer to make the adjustment from GCSE to A Level than others, and this is ok. Remember that hard work, good quality study, always pays off, and use your teachers' and your peers' feedback well to help you get to the level you want to be at, to get the grade that you need to get into the next stage of learning.

You can leave any comments on any video or the channel discussion on the *GorillaPhysics* YouTube channel, or otherwise email at kit@gorillaphysics.com. I hope you'll stop by *GorillaPhysics* on YouTube and if you feel like I can help you out in your studies, you'll become a subscriber. I'll look forward to helping you on your way to getting the grades you deserve.

Pro-tip: Take the advice and guidance of your teachers, act on feedback in a timely manner so that you can move onto the next challenge!

123

Thanks and Acknowledgements

The biggest thanks go to my YouTube community. I love making resources for you all, and I am grateful for the encouragement and support that I get from you. Honestly you inspire me, your positivity and commitment to study really keeps me going. You'll be aware that being a teacher is not an easy job, but I am blessed to have a group of young people that value my teaching which expands beyond my classroom and my department. Thanks, I really hope you find this book useful.

Thanks also to the many mentors that I have had in my career, I'd like to mention two be name. Hazel Vaughan-Dick, my chemistry teacher, teacher training mentor and first head of department, without your support I'd have struggled to see past the behaviour in my first year 9 classes to what my career could become. Secondly Helen Pollard, who, as a Institute of Physics Teaching Coach and organiser of trips and trainings, showed me the joy and importance of practical physics and of making learning experiences memorable, without your help I would not even be competent at my job! Thanks also to the many other mentors that I've not got space to mention by name, you know who you are and you've been a massive help in my career so far.

I'd like to acknowledge the many books and resources that I owe these ideas to, there are far too many to list. I hope one day another teacher gets some ideas from this book and develops them into their own resources, and recommendations to students.

Thanks also to my many students, past and present, I have been blessed with some delightful classes in all age groups. You've been the people that have tried out my ideas and study tips first, and well, you've helped me solve many problems as well, for example with apparatus, or with calculus, or just by pointing out my calculator is setup in radians!

Thankyou.

Unless stated below, images and diagrams in this book are the work of the author. Where images have been reproduced, they are either public domain, or used in good faith in accordance with the licence they were found. Every attempt has been made to comply with copyright law for this educational work, if you feel that is not the case for any image please contact the publisher using kit@gorillaphysics.com.

Cover image public domain, used with thanks:
By SpaceX [CC0 or CC0], via Wikimedia Commons

Other image credits:
A galloping horse https://commons.wikimedia.org/wiki/File:Muybridge_race_horse_gallop.jpg
AMD Ryzen Chip
https://commons.wikimedia.org/wiki/File:Zen2_Matisse_Ryzen_7nm_Core_Die_shot.jpg
The turning torso building in Malmo https://pixabay.com/photos/malm%C3%B6-turning-torso-building-3744508/
Twisted marshmallow https://www.pexels.com/photo/spiral-marshmallows-1328885/
A harmonic series of waves
https://commons.wikimedia.org/wiki/File:Harmonic_series_to_32.png
Electron Micrograph "Bedbug" http://www.freestockphotos.biz/stockphoto/16702
A car safety test
https://www.pexels.com/photo/red-and-yellow-hatchback-axa-crash-tests-163016/
Positron Discovery https://commons.wikimedia.org/wiki/File:PositronDiscovery.jpg
Trinity Test https://en.wikipedia.org/wiki/File:Trinity_Test_Fireball_16ms.jpg
A Hertzsprung-Russell diagram
https://commons.wikimedia.org/wiki/File:Sun_(PSF).png
Electron Micrograph of a bed bug
http://www.freestockphotos.biz/stockphoto/16702
Trinity Test
https://en.wikipedia.org/wiki/File:Trinity_Test_Fireball_16ms.jpg
Nuclear Stability Graph
https://commons.wikimedia.org/wiki/File:Table_isotopes_en.svg
Binding Energy Graph
https://commons.wikimedia.org/wiki/File:Binding_energy_curve_-_common_isotopes.svg
Hertzsrpung_Russell Diagram
https://www.conservapedia.com/File:Hertzsprung-Russell.jpg
NASA Local Universe Map
https://commons.wikimedia.org/wiki/File:The_Infrared_Universe.jpg
Example academic poster – Thanks to my students, they know who they are!

Printed in Great Britain
by Amazon

38167836R00072